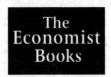

POCKET
DIRECTOR

BOB TRICKER

THE ECONOMIST IN ASSOCIATION WITH
PROFILE BOOKS LTD

Profile Books Ltd, Registered Office:
62 Queen Anne Street, London W1M 9LA

First published by Profile Books Ltd
in association with
The Economist Newspaper Ltd 1996

Typeset in Garamond by MacGuru
macguru@pavilion.co.uk

Printed in Italy by
LEGO S.p.a. – Vicenza – Italy

A CIP catalogue record for this book is available
from the British Library

ISBN 1 86197 081 1

Contents

INTRODUCTION

Being a director is one of the most challenging tasks in the modern corporate world. Once it was a sinecure: an occasional meeting with no real responsibility for a fee and maybe a lunch. Today directors are expected to perform. They are exposed to litigation and regulation. The spotlight has swung from management to the board. Managers run the business: directors ensure that is being run effectively and in the right direction.

Direction is quite different from management, yet few directors are trained for this vital role. Good managers do not necessarily make good directors. The successful director needs the ability to think strategically, to communicate effectively and to act decisively. The role calls for knowledge, experience and, above all, a tough-minded integrity.

Ultimately, the success of every enterprise depends on the calibre of its directors and the effectiveness of its board. Yet, around the world, there are some very different ideas on what the role of directors should be and how boards should be structured and run.

All these issues are explored in *Pocket Director*, which shows that the work of directors can be stimulating, challenging and creative – a far cry from the set of dry legal responsibilities often suggested.

A practical and comprehensive guide...
Pocket Director is a practical and comprehensive guide to the work of directors. It is based on sound practical knowledge of what directors really do, as well as covering what they are expected to do. Although directors all have similar responsibilities in law, in fact they play various roles in practice and make different contributions to their companies. The emphasis is on maximising individual competencies and achieving board level effectiveness.

...relevant to all...

The ideas and insights are relevant to directors of all forms of corporate entity. Directors on the boards of public companies listed on stock exchanges will find much of relevance to them; so will directors of subsidiary and associated companies operating in complex corporate groups. The particular challenges facing directors of joint-venture companies in strategic alliances are covered. Directors of family firms, large and small, will find many relevant insights; so will members of quasi-governmental boards and not-for-profit entities.

...and easy to use

Pocket Director is conveniently organised in three parts. Part 1 sets the scene with six essays on what directors really do, board structures and styles, directors' legal responsibilities, some conflicts facing directors and a review of contemporary issues. Part 2 is an A–Z of terms and ideas used internationally in discussing the work of directors and their boards. Readers will find answers to many of the common, and some not-so-common, questions that inevitably arise, together with some pertinent and a few impertinent quotations on the director's role. Part 3 has useful checklists for directors and boards, some relevant case studies and appendices with valuable additional information.

This second edition of *Pocket Director* has been substantially revised and updated to reflect developments in corporate governance thinking and practice around the world.

It is surprising that the work of potentially the most powerful group of people in any corporate entity has not featured that prominently until fairly recently. Now that it is to the fore of business considerations, I hope that you will find *Pocket Director* a useful guide to the subject of corporate governance.

Bob Tricker
July 1998

Part 1

ESSAYS

What do directors do?

What do directors do? According to conventional wisdom, directors set the strategic direction for their organisations. That is why they are called directors, after all. They appoint top management and monitor performance. Directors think rationally. They are experienced, analytical decision-makers. Directors always put the interests of the company ahead of their own. Reality suggests otherwise, however, as anyone who has ever served on or has had contact with a board of directors will know. Companies, and the boards of directors that govern them, can be strikingly different.

What directors do...

In some cases a board is intimately involved in the day-to-day running of the business, formulating its strategy, agreeing plans, allocating resources, monitoring its results and controlling its performance. In other cases a board may do little more than appoint the chief executive and rubber-stamp the proposals that come forward from management. Much depends on the governance power-base of the company and the structure and style of the board. Sometimes a board can be an administrative convenience, a legal requirement for approving decisions taken elsewhere in the organisation. Such a board might not even meet formally. But it is important to remember the work of a board can change as the circumstances facing the company change.

...and what they need to do

Figure 1 on the next page provides a simple framework for thinking about the work of directors.

Directors need to look outwards, beyond the company, seeing the business in its competitive, commercial context. They must also look inwards at the component parts of the company. They need to be able to focus on the future of the business in both the medium and the long term; and they must concentrate on the present position and

Framework for analysing board activities

	Outward looking		
Outward looking	Providing accountability		Strategy formulation
	Approve and work with and through the CEO		
Inward looking	Monitoring and supervising		Policy making
	Past and present focused		Future focused

1

recent performance.

In strategy formulation the board looks ahead in time and externally in direction, seeing the firm in its strategic environment. Then strategies need to be translated into policies that can guide top management. At the same time the board needs to monitor and supervise the activities of the executive management, looking inwards at the current managerial situation and recent performance. Finally, accountability involves looking outwards and reflecting corporate activities and performance to the shareholders as well as other stakeholders with legitimate claims to accountability. (See ACCOUNTABILITY, MONITORING MANAGEMENT and STRATEGY FORMULATION.)

The literature of management is replete with two by two matrices. The only excuse for adding yet another is this one's claim to comprehensiveness: if the directors are looking internally and externally, in the past, present and future, there is nowhere else they can look.

Finding a balance

Central to a board's work is the need to ensure that the company has the right leadership. This is shown in the centre of the quadrant. A board has to appoint, monitor and, if necessary, replace the chief executive officer (CEO). Moreover, the directors need to determine how much responsibility they want to delegate to the CEO and top management and how much they want to reserve for themselves. Boards vary considerably in the allocation of activities between the chief executive and the board as a whole.

A board also faces choices on how it allocates time and effort between the four activities. Asked about the appropriate focus of attention between the four quadrants, many directors recognise the need for more attention to the strategy formulation, top-right quadrant, but admit that short-term business pressures tend to pull the focus towards executive monitoring and supervision in the bottom-left quadrant.

Figure 1 contains a further insight into board-level activities. The left and right sides of the matrix contain fundamentally different types of activities, as shown in Figure 2. On the right, strategy formulation and policy-making are activities that contribute to the future performance of the firm, whereas those activities on the left – supervision and accountability – are about ensuring and reporting conformance to policies and plans.

The two primary functions of the board

Outward looking	Providing accountability	Strategy formulation
	CONFORMANCE	**PERFORMANCE**
Inward looking	Monitoring and supervising	Policy making
	Past and present focused	Future focused

2

In the next essay the work of unitary boards (those with both executive and non-executive directors) is contrasted with that of two-tier boards. Unitary boards undertake both the performance and the conformance responsibilities: in two-tier boards the lower board is responsible for performance, the upper or supervisory board for conformance.

Different roles for different directors

Traditionally, Anglo-American company law has not distinguished different types of directors: all directors carry the same responsibilities, whether they are executive directors or non-executive directors, whether they have some interest in the company or are totally independent outside directors. All are responsible, individually and together, for ensuring that the company is properly governed, in line with the law and for the benefit of the shareholders as a whole.

There have been suggestions recently, however, that the role and responsibilities of non-executive directors are beginning to be differentiated from those of executive directors. The findings in the 1992 AWA case (AWA Limited v Deloitte, Haskins, Sells and others) in Australia recognised that non-executive directors were not in the same position to know and take action as executive directors. The proposals in the Cadbury Report in the UK on the financial aspects of corporate governance also emphasised the role and significance of non-executive directors. Some believe that such developments would enable a court in the future to separate the responsibilities of non-executive and executive directors.

Legal responsibilities aside, there is no denying that different directors can and do make quite different (and often changing) contributions to their boards.

Defining directors' roles

In the A–Z 12 different roles have been defined, covering the principal inputs that directors can make to their boards.

Six of these roles emphasise the performance aspects of the board's work and six the conformance roles. Three of the six performance roles – wise man, specialist and window-on-the-world – are concerned with contributing knowledge, expertise and external information. The other three – figurehead, contact person and status provider – are more concerned with networking, adding status and representing the company. (See

PERFORMANCE ROLES.)

The six conformance roles – judge, catalyst, supervisor, watch dog, confidante and safety valve – are concerned with ensuring that the company follows the policies, procedures and plans the board has determined, with satisfactory results. (See CONFORMANCE ROLES.)

Most directors will play more than one role and their roles may well change over time and according to the issues before the board. However, any one director is unlikely to play all roles, because some of them conflict with others.

BOARD STRUCTURES AROUND THE WORLD

The board of directors seldom appears on the organisation chart of a company, yet it is the ultimate decision-making body. Few of the standard reference works on management and organisation draw a distinction between the work of management and of the board, yet that distinction is fundamental to understanding the work of directors. The role of management is to run the enterprise and that of the board is to see that it is being run well and in the right direction.

Typically, management operates as a hierarchy. Although the organisation may not be a neat pyramid, there is an ordering of responsibility, with authority delegated downwards through the organisation and accountability upwards to the ultimate boss, on whose desk "the buck stops". By contrast, the board should not operate as a hierarchy. Each member bears the same legal duties and responsibilities and together the members need to work as equals, reaching agreement by consensus or, if necessary, by voting.

A useful way of depicting the interaction between management and the board is to present the board as a circle superimposed on the hier-

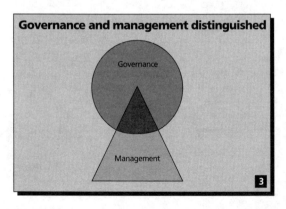

Governance and management distinguished

Governance

Management

3

archical triangle of management, as in Figure 3.

This model can be applied to the governance of any corporate entity, private or public, profit-oriented or non-profit. The circle and triangle model is a powerful analytical tool and has been used to plot complex group inter-relationships, demonstrating in whose hands power actually lies, in a way that traditional organisation structure diagrams cannot.

The significance of board structure

What is the most appropriate structure for a board of directors or the governing body of a non-profit entity? How big should the board be? What proportion of the directors should be managers in the firm? What proportion should be outside, non-executive directors? Should the chairman of the board ever also be the chief executive?

Board structure is at the foundation of board activity; board membership (the abilities, affiliations and attributes of the members) provides the driving force; and board style (the processes, powers and politics of the board) produces the effectiveness.

At its simplest, board structure distinguishes between directors who hold management positions in the company and those who do not. Those with management positions are often referred to as executive directors and those without such positions as non-executive or outside directors. (See EXECUTIVE DIRECTOR, NON-EXECUTIVE DIRECTOR, OUTSIDE DIRECTOR.)

A further distinction can be drawn between non-executive directors who are genuinely independent of the company (other than their directorship and, perhaps, a non-significant share-holding) and those who, although not employees, are in positions which might affect their independence and objectivity. For example, they may be close relations of other board members, past executives of that company, representatives of companies in the firm's added-value chain such as suppliers, agents, distributors, customers, or nominees of large equity shareholders or providers of debt capital. (See INDEPENDENT DIRECTOR.)

Although there may be good reasons for the appointment of non-executive directors with nominee or other involvement with the company, their vested interests mean that their judgment may not be totally objective. Consequently, they would not meet the check and balance requirements to be members of audit, nominating or remuneration committees. (See AUDIT COMMITTEE, NOMINATING COMMITTEE, REMUNERATION COMMITTEE.)

Structural options
In the Anglo-American traditions of corporate governance the unitary board is the norm, that is a single board made up of executive and non-executive directors in whatever proportion is thought appropriate. In the continental European model there is a two-tier board in which an upper board supervises the executive board on behalf of stakeholders.

The all-executive board
In the all-executive board every director is also a managerial employee of the company. Many start-up and family firms have this structure, with the founder, close colleagues and other family members all working in the business as well as being members of the board. The boards of some subsidiary companies operating in groups also

The all-executive board

■ Executive directors

4

choose the all-executive board, which is, in effect, the top management team of the business with no outside members. The boards of major Japanese companies are large and effectively comprise executives from the company. (See JAPANESE CORPORATE GOVERNANCE.)

The majority-executive board

In the evolution of companies and their boards, non-executive directors get appointed to boards for a number of reasons. Sometimes, in a developing private company, the executive directors feel the need for additional expertise, knowledge or skills to supplement their own. Non-executive directors can also be appointed to be nominees of those investing equity or lending money to the business, or to secure relationships with suppliers, customers or others in the added-value chain of the business. Another reason can be succession in a family firm, when shareholdings are split between branches of the family.

A potential problem of a board which is dominated by its executive directors is that they are, in effect, monitoring and supervising their own performance. One solution, other than appointing more independent non-executive directors, is for the chairman to agree with newly appointed executive directors what is expected of them. Executive directors have to wear two hats, one as the

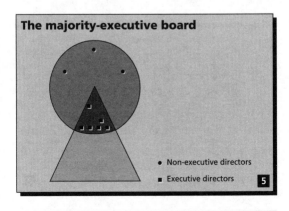

The majority-executive board

● Non-executive directors
■ Executive directors

5

manager of a part of the business, the other as a director responsible for the governance of the company. The important thing is not to be wearing the manager's hat in the boardroom.

Until recently most public companies listed in the UK had a majority of executive directors. The conventional wisdom was that "non-executive directors play an important part; there should be more than one otherwise he or she would have no power or influence (the threat of resignation would carry little weight); about a third is right but never as many as half because the company needs to be in the hands of those who are running it". Exceptions were banks and insurance companies. But attitudes are changing. In the UK the Cadbury Committee report on the financial aspects of corporate governance has been influential in emphasising the importance of independent non-executives. Consequently, the proportion of non-executive directors in British public companies has been increasing and the typical major company now has a non-executive board membership approaching 50% or higher.

The majority non-executive board
The practice of leading public companies in Australia and the United States is to have boards with a majority of non-executive directors. In many such companies the outside directors heavily out-

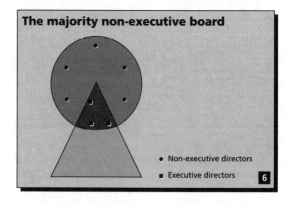

The majority non-executive board

● Non-executive directors
■ Executive directors

6

number the inside executive directors. Some argue that if the outside members dominate the board, the governance process has really ceased to be a unitary board but has moved towards the power structure of a two-tier board.

Two challenges are often thrown at outside directors: that they cannot know as much about the business as executive directors, and that the time they can devote to the company's affairs will not be sufficient. The answer to the first issue is simple: outside directors do not need to know as much about the business as the executive directors; they need to know enough to make their unique contributions. The second is an issue to be discussed before accepting the invitation to join the board. The induction checklist for directors (see Appendix 1) should prompt all the necessary questions.

The two-tier board

In the two-tier model the members of the supervisory board are totally separate from the top management team. This is the basis for corporate governance in some continental European countries. (See GERMAN CORPORATE GOVERNANCE.)

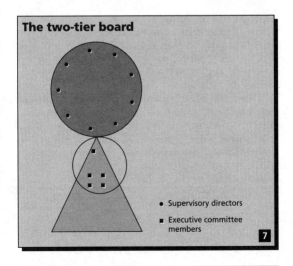

The two-tier board

• Supervisory directors
■ Executive committee members

7

Board size

The number of members on a board can have a significant bearing on its effectiveness. The chemistry of interpersonal relations at board level can be sensitive and sometimes volatile. Directors (with the exception of those appointed to rubber-stamp board decisions) are usually successful people by definition, confident by experience and strong-willed by nature. The number of board members affects the opportunity to make an impression. Too many members and meetings can become protracted. Instead of working towards consensus, divisions may arise and cabals emerge, resulting in adversarial voting. On the other hand, with too few members there may be a shortage of the necessary talents, knowledge and experience.

Maximum and minimum numbers are often prescribed in the company's articles of association and can be amended by the shareholders. Interestingly, a case is often made for increasing the size of the board, seldom for reducing it. Yet as companies evolve situations can arise when a smaller board might be more effective.

In Japan boards can be extremely large. (See JAPANESE CORPORATE GOVERNANCE.)

Groups of companies

Major companies almost always operate in groups. Some are reasonably simple hierarchies of wholly and partly owned subsidiaries). Others involve complex networks with hundreds of subsidiary and associated companies.

Directors of companies within such groups may face the problem of "dual lines of control". As directors their duty is to act in the best interests of the shareholders, which, if the subsidiary is wholly owned by the parent company, may not cause too many problems. If, however, there are minority interests in the company, perhaps a joint-venture partner or a strategic ally, executive directors might find themselves having to choose between what is in the best interests of the company and what is in their interests as executives of the main group. (See REPRESENTATIVE DIRECTOR.)

MAKING A BOARD EFFECTIVE

Although the chairman is often called the "chairman of the company", he or she is in reality the chairman of the board. The articles of association of many companies provide for the directors to appoint one of their number to the chair. In other words, the chairman is elected as a director by the shareholders in general meeting, but appointed to the chairmanship by the other directors.

In major companies, however, the role of the chairman has tended to expand to include not only the management of the board meetings (determining the agenda, chairing the meetings and agreeing the minutes), but also a wider responsibility for board matters, such as reviewing board performance and director development. In other cases the chairman takes on a role as a major spokesman for the company, relieving the chief executive officer of such chores.

A long-running debate is whether one person should combine the roles of chief executive and chairman. Those who call for wider conformance from boards say that to split the functions provides necessary checks and balances, and avoids domination by one person. Others point to companies that have been successful because they have been dominated by entrepreneurial figures. They further argue that circumstances can arise when performance issues outweigh conformance issues and tough-minded, single leadership is essential. In Australia and the UK the tendency in major, listed companies is for the roles to be separated, although there are well-known cases of joint roles. In the United States the roles are frequently combined, which has led to criticism from institutional investor organisations that the top executive has too much power. (See DUALITY.)

Board styles

The chairman of the board inevitably has an effect on the way that the board goes about its business. Boards vary enormously. Figure 8 depicts four different board styles, indicating the extent of the directors' concern for their interpersonal relationships at board level, on the one hand, and their tough-minded concern for the work of the board, on the other.

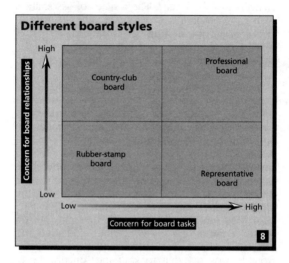

Different board styles

Concern for board relationships

High

Low

Country-club board

Professional board

Rubber-stamp board

Representative board

Low ──────────────▶ High

Concern for board tasks

8

Rubber stamps The directors of a rubber-stamp style board have little concern for either the tasks of the board or the interpersonal relationships among the directors. Examples of such boards can be found in the "letter-box" companies registered in many offshore tax havens. The meetings of the board are a formality. Indeed they are often minuted without them actually taking place. The boards of some closely held private companies also treat their board meetings as a formality; perhaps because one individual is dominant and takes the decisions, or because the key players see each other frequently and decisions are taken in the management context.

Country clubs The country-club board is concerned with interpersonal relations at board level, even if the focus on the issues before the board takes second place. The boards of some old companies, which have been successful in the past, fit this model. There is likely to be a great deal of ritual about board meetings. The boardroom will be beautifully furnished, complete with pictures of previous chairmen. Long-established traditions are revered. Innovation is discouraged.

Representative boards The representative board places more emphasis on the tasks of the board than it does on board relations. It frequently has directors representing different shareholders or stakeholders and is more like a parliament of diverse interests. Issues can easily become politicised. Discussions can be adversarial. The basis and balance of power is important. The governing bodies (councils, committees, boards, and so on) of many not-for-profit charitable, educational and cultural entities fit this model.

Professional boards The professional board shows concern for both the board's tasks and its interpersonal relationships. A board with a successful professional style will have sound leadership from the chair. There will be tough-minded discussion among the members combined with a mutual understanding and respect for each other.

Reviewing effectiveness
There is a danger that the board of a successful company can become complacent and its style of leadership in the boardroom, once so suitable, no longer appropriate. A business can outgrow its board. But change is difficult to achieve. There is a need for a strategy for board-level development. The board effectiveness review checklist in Appendix 3 will enable a board's current structure and style to be analysed. Alternatives can be devised, evaluated and discussed in the context of the business strategy. Then a strategy for developing the board and its members can evolve in line with, and as part of, the ongoing strategies to develop the company as a whole.

DIRECTORS' LEGAL DUTIES AND RESPONSIBILITIES

The principal responsibility of directors is to the members of the company, that is the equity shareholders. In almost all jurisdictions two basic ideas underlie directors' duties: that they act with probity; and that they exercise reasonable care, diligence and skill.

Honesty, integrity and candour

The primary duty of a director is to act honestly in good faith for the benefit of all of the shareholders, giving them equal, sufficient and accurate information on all issues that could affect their interests. Directors may not treat the company as though it exists for their personal benefit. Even in the case of the "closed" company, in which the owners, the directors and the management are the same people, the company is an independent entity and the rights of other parties, such as the creditors and the state, need to be respected by the board.

A director must not make a secret profit out of dealings with the company. Any such interests must be disclosed to the board. For example, if a director is associated with another company whose tender for a major contract is being considered by the board, this interest must be disclosed. The board might decide that there is no problem and ask the director to refrain from comment or voting on the matter, or even ask the director to leave the room while it is being discussed. Having declared an interest, directors would be wise to ensure that it has been minuted, in case it is raised in the future.

Insider trading, that is dealing in the shares of a quoted company on the basis of information that is price-sensitive and obtained in a privileged way as a director, is improper. Indeed, in almost all jurisdictions it is now a criminal offence, although in some places there have been few prosecutions because of the difficulties of obtaining reliable evidence.

In practice, this fiduciary duty to act in the interests of the company as a whole can prove difficult for directors. Take a typical example. Warren Bishop was nominated by the finance house for which he worked to serve on the board of a start-up company. The finance house had subscribed for 25% of the equity capital plus a major loan, convertible to equity in the future. Mr Bishop attended board meetings assiduously and followed the development of the company's business with great care. He fully appreciated the cash-flow difficulties that faced the company in its first few years. But he found himself in a difficult situation. As a director, concerned for the shareholders as a whole, he knew the company must have additional funds to fund working capital. As a representative of the finance house, however, he did not feel able to recommend that they risk additional funds, even though that would put the future of the company in jeopardy. Such dilemmas frequently occur where there are representative or nominee directors. (See REPRESENTATIVE DIRECTOR.) Another case can arise with directors serving on the board of a joint-venture company, when conflicts of interest arise between those of the joint venture and the partner organisation for whom they work. (See STRATEGIC ALLIANCES.)

Nevertheless, boards must take decisions in good faith for the common good of all shareholders. Commonwealth-based company law tends to allow directors to determine the best interests of them all as a whole, subject to the right of appeal to the courts. Directors of companies incorporated in most US states owe specific duties to minority shareholders.

Care, diligence and skill

A further overall duty imposed on directors, by statute and case law depending on the jurisdiction, is the duty to exercise reasonable care, diligence and skill in their work as directors. The interpretation of what constitutes reasonable skill and care varies among countries and has been changing over time.

In the past, for example, in the UK a directorship was not an onerous task. An occasional meeting, a few questions, an expression of interest and support, for a fee and, perhaps, a lunch, was often all that was required. This has now changed. Legal actions have been brought against companies, boards and, in some cases, individual directors alleging negligence, abuses of power or infringement of the rights of minority shareholders. Moreover, the courts have extended their expectations of what can reasonably be expected of a director.

Directors do not need to be lawyers or accountants to fulfil their legal responsibilities, but it is wise for them to be briefed on such matters to ensure that they know when to seek advice. Obviously, directors with professional qualifications can reasonably be expected to act with the skill and care of experts in their fields. But more and more is now expected of all directors, including those who do not have professional qualifications.

The board of directors is the overall decision-making body in the modern corporation. The directors carry the ultimate responsibility for everything the company does. Yet most directors, and there are millions of them around the world, have never had any formal training for their work. The majority are unaware of the growing body of knowledge that is now available about the work of directors, board-level effectiveness and the exercise of power of the modern corporate entity – what is now called corporate governance. There are similarities to the position of managers in the 1950s, before the growth of management training, management theories and business schools.

The standard of professionalism expected of directors around the world is significantly higher than a few years ago and rising. Courts are increasingly prepared to act if fraudulent or negligent behaviour by directors is alleged, or where there seem to be abuses of power by directors or infringements of minority rights. Many company regulators around the world have also acquired new powers and shown their willingness to act. For example, in the UK the number of people being disqualified from being a company director has increased significantly. Business decision-making, however, involves making judgments and taking risks, and it is not the role of the courts to second guess commercial judgments made by directors, even though with hindsight they turn out to have been misguided.

Corporate effectiveness

What has been said so far is, broadly, relevant to the directors of all companies, but particularly those of public, listed companies. The basis of power in some other types of company can influence the basis of corporate governance and affect the responsibilities of directors.

Subsidiary and associate companies Directors of companies operating within groups – including wholly and partly owned subsidiaries, associated companies in which another company holds less than a controlling but nevertheless a dominating interest, and companies in strategic alliances – can find themselves in special circumstances.

Difficulties can arise if control over the group of companies is exercised through group-wide organisation and management control systems, rather than through the governance structure of each company. If the subsidiary is wholly owned, whether a decision is made through group organisational channels or through the governance structures may not matter much in the long term because the group top executives are also acting as shareholders. But where there are outside, minority interests in a company, directors can face problems.

Consider an example. John Write was the managing director of a subsidiary company in a British group of diverse companies. The group had acquired his company from family interests some years earlier. About 18% of the shares of the subsidiary were still in the hands of family members. Mr Write realised that he had a duty towards these minority shareholders, but he also had a duty to the group as the major shareholder. More significantly, he was also an employee of the group which determined his remuneration and promotion prospects. All went well until the group head office decided on a change of strategy. The products of the subsidiary company, it was felt, were in decline and, rather than invest in product innovation, it was decided to treat the company as a "cash cow", deny it further investment and "milk" it in order to start up new ventures elsewhere in the group. Mr Write faced a dilemma: how could he reconcile his duty to the group, which employed him, and his duty to the minority shareholders of the subsidiary company, of which he was a director? In the end the board of the majority holding company had to strike a compromise with the minority holders in the subsidiary company.

Strategic alliances In recent years alliances between companies have become widespread as a strategic response to product innovation, procurement, production, marketing, or financing needs. Directors of companies created in such situations can face some similar conflicts.

For example, Jean Williams was appointed by her company, a major US telecommunications organisation operating around the world, to the board of a joint-venture company whose shares were held 60% by her company and 40% by a Japanese group. The strategic alliance had been formed to manufacture electronic components in Thailand and China, using technology developed by the Japanese and the distribution channels of the US group. Unfortunately, after three successful years of operation, the Japanese partners felt that changes in manufacturing technology and in the market necessitated a fundamental change in the product pricing structures, which would have been to the detriment of the US owner. This was a situation not foreseen in the original joint-venture agreement. Ms Williams was in a difficult position.

As a director of the associated company she knew that her duty was to this company and both of its shareholders. She could see the Japanese firm's point of view but she also had a loyalty towards the US company that employed her. Her difficulties were compounded by the threat of litigation by the Japanese firm if she disclosed information given to her as a director of the associated company to her American bosses. In the event the joint-venture company was wound up.

Family companies In the family company another set of issues can arise for directors. Initially, corporate governance is often dominated by the founder who is also chairman and chief executive. Inside directors are closely related to the founder and outside directors, if they exist, have usually been invited to add knowledge, skills and experience that are not otherwise available on the board. But on succession real problems can arise, particularly if inheritance has split the shareholding between family members who are still involved in management and those who are not.

Consider another example. A prosperous family company, manufacturing and retailing furniture in the Midwest of the United States, was run by the son and daughter of the founder, each of whom held 25% of the shares. Another 25% of the equity was held by their brother, a lawyer in San Francisco, and the remainder by a cousin who lived in France. The family members with executive positions naturally wanted to enhance their remuneration and benefits, arguing that it was their work that was producing the performance. The outside shareholders, however, resented the rewards being taken by the incumbent executive directors. "Why should they give themselves these fancy cars, high salaries and expensive trips abroad?" they asked. "The original directors never spent that much on themselves." Another problem for the directors arose when other family members expected early promotion to top management posts, whereas the business had reached the stage of growth and complexity which desperately needed executives with professional qualifications and experience that the sons and daughters of the family lacked. The power struggles at board level became a particular problem for the chief executive, who was also the chairman. He tried to resolve them by appointing independent outside directors to advise him, but could not avoid a family feud.

Corporatised and privatised companies In recent years there has been a trend throughout the Western world of corporatising (making state-owned businesses more like companies in the private sector) or privatising (selling off all or part of the business to the private sector) such state entities as power, water and transport utilities and telecommunications companies.

Directors of such companies face unique problems. In the corporatised quasi-government entity there is the question of who should appoint the directors since the state remains the sole shareholder. Political issues can arise; for example, in privatised companies should the state retain a voting majority of the equity or a "golden share", to ensure that the strategically important interests of the country do not fall into the wrong hands? How is performance to be determined since, in many cases, there remains a degree of monopoly in the supply of services? Then there is the matter of social costs. In many utilities, if market forces were to be given a free rein, consumers who are poor or who live in remote areas might suffer. Mechanisms to regulate market prices are often introduced. All these issues affect the responsibilities of directors of such quasi-government companies.

Non-profit corporate entities Finally, there are the directors of non-profit enterprises, sometimes incorporated as companies limited by guarantee. It is possible that directors of such enterprises will also be bound by legislation designed to regulate charities and other non-profit entities. They might also find themselves in the position of trustees. However, the fundamental duties to act with honesty, integrity and candour, and to exercise care, diligence and skill still apply. But, by definition, non-profit companies lack the profit basis for measuring performance. Consequently, a particular challenge to the boards of such entities is to determine the precise mission of the corporate entity and the criteria by which success is to be measured. Balancing the pursuit of multiple objectives and satisfying the expectations of a range of stakeholders, in both the long and the short term, can be difficult.

THE CORPORATE GOVERNANCE DEBATE

The directors' role is integral to the concept of the corporation. Although company law varies from country to country, there are some general points that can usefully be made.

The concept of the company

The original concept of the company was immensely innovative, elegantly simple and proved to be superbly successful. In the middle of the 19th century, apart from companies created by the state or the crown, the only way to do business was as a sole trader or a partnership. If the business became insolvent, the proprietor went to the debtors' prison and his family to the workhouse; hardly an incentive for an investor to risk his funds in a venture run by others. Yet extra finance was exactly what the businesses growing out of the industrial revolution needed. So the concept of the corporation was created.

In the joint stock, limited liability company the business is incorporated as an independent legal entity, separate from its owners, whose liability for its debts is limited to the amount of equity capital they have agreed to subscribe. A corporate veil is thus drawn round the company, which has many of the rights of a legal person: to buy and sell, to own assets, to incur debts, to employ, to contract and to sue and be sued.

The company has a life of its own. Although this does not guarantee perpetuity, it does give the company an existence independent of the life of the proprietors, who can transfer their shares to others.

Ownership is the basis of power over the company (at least in the Western world): power to nominate and elect the directors, who run the enterprise on behalf of the shareholders; power to require accountability from the directors, the stewards of the business's resources; and power to question them on their report and financial accounts. The members also have independent auditors (in the early days appointed from among themselves) to report that these accounts show a true and fair view of the state of affairs of the company.

The UK adopts company laws

At the beginning of the 19th century to separate a business from its owners would have been thought foolhardy and to restrict the responsibility of owners for their debts immoral. By the end of the century both were commonplace. In 1844 in the UK, the world's leading industrial nation at the time, Parliament passed a Joint Stock Companies Act calling for registration of incorporated companies. In 1855 an act was passed which limited the liability of shareholders. This was followed by a consolidating act in 1862.

British influence in the succeeding years around the world meant that these notions became the basis of company law and corporate governance in many places including the Australian states, the Canadian provinces, Hong Kong, India, New Zealand, Singapore and South Africa. Their company law remains linked through the British Commonwealth, but its extent now varies significantly among jurisdictions. The Companies Act, for example, in Hong Kong runs to less than 400 pages, in Singapore to nearer 600 and in the UK to about 700. At the other extreme, the company law of the British Virgin Islands, a tax haven that has attracted many companies to incorporate because of its undemanding regulatory regime, covers just 100 pages.

The United States follows

Company law developments in the United States evolved along similar lines and reflected similar ideological traditions. Individual states passed legislation to facilitate the incorporation of companies. Governance was again through the meeting of shareholder members in the company. Incorporation of companies at the federal level was not and is still not available, although federal government does exercise power over securities trading through the Securities and Exchange Commission.

Continental Europe goes its own way

Developments in continental Europe followed a different path, reflecting different cultural norms. Companies in Germany, for example, were more heavily regulated and lacked the flexibility of the Anglo-American model. Shareholders' interests are protected by a board of supervision, quite separate from the management of the business. The supervisory board examines and reports on the accounts prepared by the managers. They can call meetings of the shareholders and can, if necessary, change the managers. Top management are thus potentially under greater scrutiny than their Anglo-American counterparts. (See TWO-TIER BOARD and GERMAN CORPORATE GOVERNANCE.)

In France the 1807 Napoleonic Code provided the basis for company law. The *société en commandité par actions* was a form of incorporation in which the liability of the managing directors for corporate debts was unlimited while the liability of the outside investors was limited to their equity stake. The *société à responsabilité limitée* was introduced in 1863, giving limited liability to both managing and outside shareholders.

Fundamental differences in company law still survive in Europe, despite the efforts of the European Union's harmonisation programme. The social programme is now being used to impose a degree of regulation, in matters such as worker representation, on companies trading in EU member states.

Anglo-Saxon roots

Thus the original concept of the company is rooted in Anglo-Saxon ideology. The importance attached to the notion of the individual, emphasising personal freedoms and self-regulation under the common law, had a medieval root which contrasted with the more prescriptive rule of law in the continental European jurisdictions which relied on Roman legal traditions.

Different cultures, different opinions
Opinions differ on what the content and boundaries of corporate governance should be. For some the essence is the exercise of power by shareholders; for others it is formal structures of the board and corporate effectiveness that matter; yet others believe the focus should be on the social responsibilities of corporations to a wider set of stakeholders. This book takes the view that corporate governance is concerned with the structure and processes of the board and its relationships with shareholders, regulators, auditors, top management and any other legitimate stakeholders. Figure 9 illustrates the scope of corporate governance in a limited liability company.

Corporate governance in a limited liability company

Philip Cochran and Steven Wartick, two American scholars writing in 1988, suggested that:

Corporate governance is an umbrella term that includes specific issues arising from interactions among senior management, shareholders, boards of directors, and other corporate stakeholders.

There have been a number of calls for fundamentally rethinking the concept of the corporation. A well-known British management writer, Charles Handy, has recently questioned why ownership was the basis of power in the corporation. "How and why did the concept of property ever enter the debate?" he has asked, offering the alternative of the company as a self-governing, wealth-creating community. But back in 1932 two American researchers, Adolph Berle and Gardiner Means, showed the separation of ownership from control that was occurring, with power concentrated in the hands of management rather than shareholders of large US public companies. Yet most companies' law around the world still assumes a shareholders' democracy as in the 19th century.

Theories of corporate governance

There are five main theories relating to corporate governance.

Stewardship theory Underpinning company law is the requirement that directors show a fiduciary duty towards the shareholders of the company. Inherent in this idea is the belief that the directors can be trusted. Stewardship theory reflects these classical ideas of corporate governance. Power over the corporation is exercised through directors, who are nominated and appointed by the shareholders in general meeting and who are accountable to them for the stewardship over the company's resources, subject to a report to the members from an independent auditor that their accounts show a true and fair view. Stewardship theory remains the theoretical foundation for much regulation and legislation.

Organisation theory was relatively slow to focus on issues at the corporate governance level. In practice, the board of directors was superimposed on few organisation charts; in theory, most organisational studies seemed to assume that organisation structures peaked with the CEO. In recent years, however, there have been some important contributions from the psychology of behavioural and leadership studies and the sociology of organisational and managerial work.

Stakeholder theory emerged during the 1970s, reflecting a fear at the societal level that the large, particularly multinational, corporation had become too large and powerful to be held accountable solely through the classical stewardship mode. Ralph Nader, a passionate advocate of consumer rights in the USA, argued:

> *(Giant corporations) can spend decisive amounts to determine which towns thrive and which gather cobwebs, corrupt or help overthrow foreign governments, develop technology that takes lives or saves lives… (The giant corporation) is largely unaccountable to its constituencies – shareholders, workers, consumers, local communities, taxpayers, small businesses, future generations.*

In 1975 the Accounting Standards Steering Committee in the UK produced a discussion paper recommending that all economic entities should provide regular accountability reports to all stakeholder groups whose interests might be affected by the decisions of the entity. The political implications of such a heroic idea quickly relegated the report to the files. During the growth and greed era of the 1980s little was heard of stakeholder theories, but in the more environmentally and socially concerned world of the 1990s the ideas are reappearing, for example with socially aware mutual funds.

Agency theory has been a contribution of the 1980s to corporate governance thinking. Although derived from the work of an American economist, Ronald Coase, in the 1930s, the ideas of agency theory have been applied to directors and boards only in recent years. Inherent in this theoretical perspective is a different view of the nature of man: that he is self-interested rather than altruistic, and that he cannot always be trusted to act in the best interests of others but, rather, to maximise his own utility.

Agency theory presents the relationship between the directors and the shareholders as a contract. Because the directors (the agents) will take decisions in their own interests, the transaction costs of check and balance mechanisms, such as further disclosure, independent outside directors and audit committees of the board, should be incurred to the point at which the reduction of the loss from non-compliance equals the increase in enforcement costs.

Theory of the firm Agency theory and the related transaction-cost economics have become an important component of financial economics and the so-called theory of the firm. A fierce academic debate is still going on between the agency theorists and the stewardship theorists. The former argue that their models are sound and their results statistically revealing; the latter maintain that the same data can be reworked to show opposite effects.

Cultural conundrum
There is, however, another perspective. Stewardship theory, stakeholder theory and agency theory are all essentially ethnocentric. Although the underlying ideological paradigms are seldom articulated, the essential ideas are derived from Western thought, with its perceptions and expectations of the respective roles of individual, enterprise and state and of the relationships between them. But what of other cultures with different perceptions of governance power? (See CHINESE CORPORATE GOVERNANCE and JAPANESE CORPORATE GOVERNANCE.)

Whose company is it anyway?
Implicit in the concept of the joint stock, limited liability company is the belief that ownership provides the basis of power over the corporation. The

corporate entity is run for the benefit of the shareholders. Meeting together on a properly convened
occasion, the shareholders nominate and elect the
directors. Stewardship over the company is exercised by the directors for the benefit of the shareholders. The directors demonstrate their
accountability to the shareholders through regular
reports and audited financial statements. Such is
the conventional wisdom and the legal fiction.

Even in the 19th century it is doubtful if the
reality approached this ideal of shareholder
democracy, and at the end of the 20th century the
unreality is apparent. In the early days of the
corporate concept company promoters could, and
many did, wield significant power. But at least in
those days shareholders were comparatively few
and drawn from the ranks of the emerging *rentier*
class of the relatively wealthy. They tended to be
socially and geographically concentrated. They
actually attended shareholders' meetings.

Today the concept of shareholder democracy
has become an anachronism. Individual shareholders are unable to exercise any significant
influence, unless they have a sufficient shareholding to be dominant. There are exceptions, of
course. In family companies, where owners,
directors and managers are often the same people
or are closely intertwined, ownership power can
be meaningful in influencing board appointments
and determining corporate strategies. In subsidiary and associated companies operating in
groups or strategic alliance networks, ownership
power can be effective, even though control (and
power) is often exercised through group organisational control systems not governance mechanisms. Even in public listed companies the power
of the proxy vote becomes real should the company be "put into play" through an attempted hostile takeover.

But the conventional wisdom that shareholders
determine board membership and can influence
corporate direction is, by and large, false; certainly
in major public listed companies. Yet commentators continue to call on shareholders to "exercise

their power". What power? Commenting on the need to control allegedly excessive director remuneration, the Greenbury Report calls on investors to "use their power and influence" to ensure the implementation of the code of best practice the committee has proposed.

It has been clear for many years, around the commercially advanced world, that individual small shareholders have no real power in governance matters. In the major listed companies shareholdings are widely dispersed and geographically spread. Even with shareholder interest groups and better opportunities to communicate with the other members, individual investors lack the position, prestige or power to influence an incumbent chairman and his or her board.

Institutional muscle

Institutional investors, however, do appear to have some power to influence boards, particularly if they act in concert. But this presupposes that the interests of institutional investors are homogeneous, which they are not. The time horizon, risk profile and the interests of the stakeholders of pension funds can be quite different from those of mutual funds and different again from the interests of financial institutions offering private services to wealthy investors. In any case the fund manager voting such shares has already removed the ultimate beneficiary by at least one level from personal shareholder democracy. Moreover, the fund managers of some financial institutions, particularly insurance funds, may have difficulty in voting the shares of some of their holdings.

Certainly institutional investor pressure, such as that exerted by Pension Investment Research Consultants (PIRC) in the UK and Calpers (the Californian State Employees pension fund) in the United States, has been influential in sharpening up boardroom attitudes. The removal of the chairmen and boards of under-performing companies in recent years, including American Express, IBM and General Motors, makes the point. But such institutional pressure has not (at least in the short term) always benefited the shareholders. In the case of Saatchi & Saatchi, the removal of the dominant entrepreneur resulted in him setting up a competing firm, taking significant accounts with him, and a decline in the share price of the original firm (renamed Cordiant) that the shareholder action was supposed to address.

Relationship investing, in which the institutional investor takes a major stake and a long-term interest in return for a seat on the board and therefore a chance to influence board decisions, might be seen to offer a greater chance of shareholder influence. But again there is no guarantee that what is good for investors such as Warren Buffett or Robert Monks is consistent with the goals of the other shareholders. Relationship investing is not a return to shareholder democracy.

In fairness, the attempts by the boards of some major firms to communicate with their shareholders should be acknowledged. Shareholder meetings in various locations, an array of publications, company information on the Internet, videos of annual meetings, invitations to meet and question the directors: these are all attempts to inform those with an interest in the company. But it should be remembered that they are also intended to maintain shareholder support and to influence share prices positively, a valuable operation if raising new funds – and for those who have executive share options they want to exercise.

Time for change

It is clear that the 19th century concept of the corporation, based on ownership power, has become inadequate. But as we approach the 21st century other problems have arisen. Modern settlement systems leave the investments of small shareholders in nominee companies. How are these shares to be voted? Huge sums of money are also being invested in warrants and other forms of derivative instruments, so the ultimate owners are yet further removed from voting power over the corporate entities in which the investments are based. Who is now to exercise power over companies?

The way ahead

Perhaps the way ahead is to face up to the reality. Shareholders can, at best, influence corporate behaviour; they can no longer wield overall governance power. Power lies with the incumbent board. The ultimate power is the right to nominate and appoint to that board.

So the crucial question becomes: who should wield the power to appoint directors, and by what mechanisms? A nominating committee made up of independent outside directors is the current preferred response. But even if nominating committees of independent non-executive directors are created, might they not reflect the interests of the board incumbents, who nominated them and with whom they have to work, rather than the interests of the shareholders?

Creating a nominating committee begs the question: who chooses the outside directors on the nominating committee? Might they not form a cosy club of like-minded executives from other companies, perhaps with cross-directorships? As Juvenal, a Roman satirist and poet, said: "*Quis custodiet ipsos custodes?*" (Who will guard the guards?) But then he was worried about those he had set to guard his wife as he went off to war. A shareholder committee, perhaps? But how to produce a slate of genuine alternatives? Candidate manifestos? Now we are back to the stakeholder arguments of the 1970s. A separate shareholder supervisory committee? A two-tier board?

It is very unlikely that an ideal solution exists, but the next few years are likely to produce some revolutionary new thinking on the role of boards and the work of their directors. Nothing less than a complete reinvention of the 19th century, Western concept of the corporation is likely to suffice: one that does not merely treat companies as either private or public, but that can reflect the reality of governance power in complex group chains and networks, strategic alliances and cross-held corporate entities.

Issues facing directors

Corporate governance is about the exercise of power over corporate entities. At the beginning of the 1980s the term corporate governance was seldom used; today it is commonplace. Around the world issues of corporate governance are exciting the interest of academics and professionals alike; even the popular press carries commentaries on the subject. In the United States, the removal of dominant chief executives has been brought about by pressure from institutional investors, dissatisfied with their companies' strategic direction. Relationship investing suggests closer links between institutional shareholders and management. In the UK the Stock Exchange has produced principles of corporate governance and codes of best practice, consolidating the recommendations of the Cadbury (1992), Greenbury (1995) and Hampel (1998) committees. Similar codes of conduct have also been developed for other jurisdictions. Around the world accountability for allegedly excessive director remuneration has become a concern. Nor are the issues of governance limited to the public company. Privatisation and corporatisation of entities previously in the public domain have added a new set of issues. Top management succession gives many family firms their share of governance problems. In the modern world, even the non-profit sector – universities, cultural societies, professional institutions, for example – seems to have its share of problems at the level of the governing body.

Company law and regulation

The body of company law in the jurisdiction in which the company is incorporated, and sometimes where it does business, determines many of the responsibilities faced by directors in that state or country. Further duties may arise from the laws of insolvency, consumer protection, monopoly and merger control, employment, environmental protection and so on. For the director of a public company, whose shares are traded on a stock exchange, the laws of securities trading and investor protection also apply, as well as the rules of the specific stock exchange itself.

Trends
Two trends are affecting directors' responsibilities around the world.

1 Legislators are increasing the statutory requirements regulating companies and requiring disclosure of corporate affairs. Moreover, there are forces encouraging the convergence of securities regulation and corporate governance rules under the auspices of the International Organisation of Securities Commissions (IOSCO), whose membership includes most of the world's securities regulatory bodies, from the Securities and Exchange Commission in the United States to the Securities and Futures Commission in Hong Kong. IOSCO members have agreed to exchange information on unusual trades, thus making global insider trading easier to detect.

The International Accounting Standards Committee and the International Auditing Practices Committee of the International Federation of Accountants also have close links with the IOSCO and are further forces working towards international harmonisation and standardisation of financial reporting and auditing practices.

2 Shareholders and other parties feeling aggrieved about the way the directors have been running companies have increasingly been resorting to litigation. The lead came from the United States, where the contingent fee system (whereby lawyers are paid a percentage of whatever damages are awarded or agreed) and class actions (that is the possibility of joining all the members of a specific class, such as shareholders, in a claim without their specific consent) is widely believed to have encouraged litigation. But other countries, including Australia, Canada and the UK, have also seen an increase in actions brought against companies, boards, individual directors and the companies' auditors.

Insurance cover for negligence or other claims against directors and other company officials has proved increasingly necessary and premiums have risen accordingly. Indeed, there are a growing number of cases in which prominent people have refused directorships because of the exposure, not only to the threat of litigation and financial costs, but also to the media interest and personal approbation that can follow a legal action, even if successfully defended.

Directors' remuneration

If the corporate governance *cri de coeur* of the 1980s was occasioned by the excesses of predators and the paraphernalia of poison pills, greenmail, white knights and the rest, the clamour of the 1990s so far has been about allegedly excessive board-level remuneration and the associated rolling contracts, share options and golden handshakes. In the UK, where directors' rewards continue to outstrip inflation and pay awards to other staff, the media have led the debate, but institutional investors have also been challenging board-level compensation.

Directors' contracts The effect of rolling contracts for directors, of course, is to boost the payoff for directors whose contracts are terminated (or who follow the face-saving formula of "retiring" by agreement). The Cadbury Committee recommended that two years should be the maximum period for such contracts and most UK listed companies have complied, although a few rewarded their directors with a payment for the loss of a contractual benefit. The shareholders of a number of major companies have been challenging the rolling three-year contracts enjoyed by their directors. The National Association of Pension Funds, having sought the views of its members, seems to think that rolling contracts should be limited to no more than one year and any fixed-term contracts should not be for more than three years.

Share options The intention of share options is inherently sound: to reward good performance by linking director remuneration to improvements in the share price. Unfortunately, there are major drawbacks. For one thing, share option schemes tend to reward general rises in the market that are unrelated to the performance of the company itself; for another, poor performance that pulls the share price down carries no penalty.

Privatised particulars In the UK privatised utilities have come in for particular criticism. In many cases with near monopoly markets, top management have become millionaires, not because they built up the business through their entrepreneurial flair, nor because of personal risk or any special contribution to performance, but because they happened to be in the right place at the right time. High salaries, generous share options and contract termination provisions have all been criticised.

The going rate Arguments advanced to support high remuneration levels are the need to attract the best people and to retain existing directors. Comparisons with levels of reward in other countries is also often cited in justification. Other arguments include the need for comparability with similar companies and with the professions (such as the lawyers and auditors to the company), and to maintain differentials with non-board senior executive staff. Comparability with the rewards of stars of the sporting and entertainment worlds is less easy to sustain; but comparisons with top military personnel, and the staff of the United Nations, World Bank and European Union can provide some indicators.

Towards a solution

There are three potential levels of control.

Self-control at the board level This is crucial, and includes the influence of independent non-executive directors, particularly those who serve on the remuneration committee of the board, if there is one. But since so many outside directors are themselves top executives and directors of other companies, the fear of mutual back-scratching is always present. The Cadbury and Hampel Committees emphasised the importance of non-executive directors and, like the Greenbury Report, recommended remuneration committees, requiring listed companies to state whether they had one and to explain the formula by which they worked. The separation of the CEO role from that of the board chairman could also provide a counter to remuneration policies dominated by the CEO – an idea that could be particularly pertinent in the United States.

Influence at shareholder level Shareholders are hampered by having to rely on the information they are given in, for example, the directors' report and the audited accounts. The absence of details of directors' contracts makes argument difficult, particularly in general meetings that are dominated by a chairman with proxy votes to hand. A stronger potential lies with the institutional investors, although a spokesman for the National Association of Pension Funds in the UK has pointed out that "the sums involved (in directors' remuneration) are often 'flea-bites' as far as the earnings of most big companies are concerned ... fund managers are interested in share price and profits performance not what directors pay themselves". A suggestion from Australia is for a corporate senate, elected by shareholders, to reflect their interests (see CORPORATE SENATE). Relationship investing in which institutional investors take a significant, long-term stake in a company could be more influential.

Control at the societal level Social disapproval, often expressed through the media, can affect attitudes. Tim Melville-Ross, director-general of the influential Institute of Directors in London, has said: "I am perfectly happy about the idea of real entrepreneurs who take big risks taking away substantial rewards. But for bureaucrats to be similarly rewarded is wrong." Stockmarket regulators or fund managers might develop exhortatory guidelines. As a matter of political judgment, governments could introduce tax disincentives or even legal sanctions and mandatory limits.

What's right?
The real issue is not so much how to design mechanisms that regulate and control directors' remuneration, but how to determine the "right" amount that will reward contribution and risk, and will control greed and avoid envy. In other words, to decide what is fair and reasonable and is seen to be so. Bill Gates, CEO of Microsoft, one of the most successful companies in the United States, is one of the lowest-paid CEOs in corporate America. Of course his holding in the company he created has made him one of the richest men in the United States. What are needed now are some benchmarks that relate reward to long-term performance.

New complexities
A final area of conflict in corporate governance arises as a result of the complexity of structures now being adopted in international business. Single corporate entities are a thing of the past, except in small and family firms. Instead there are complex networks of subsidiary and associated companies, cross-holdings, public companies with chained ownership giving leveraged power to those at the top, private companies and limited partnerships controlling public listed companies, and many other forms of strategic alliances which have changed the power relationship from that envisaged in the original corporate concept.

Power base
The essence of governance is power. A British Labour prime minister, Harold Wilson, in his book *The Governance of Britain,* wrote of the power to govern at the level of the state. Corporate governance is the exercise of power at the level of the corporate entity. In the 19th century, when the brilliantly innovative concept of the joint stock,

limited liability company was conceived, ownership was the undisputed basis of power. So it still is in most jurisdictions according to company law. But how different is the reality.

Today power over a corporation can lie with several, often competing, groups of people. Institutional investors have rediscovered the ability to influence corporate affairs, particularly in the United States where the former chairmen of some major corporations rue the institutions' new-found powers. Relationship investors aim to wield power through a significant and long-term commitment to the corporation. In Germany power on the supervisory board is shared between labour and capital. In the Netherlands it is a tripartite relationship between capital, labour and the public interest. France permits a number of alternative power bases. In Japan the powers behind the *keiretsu* wield the power. In China the state still seeks to exercise an influence over corporate entities.

Cadbury stirred it up...

The Cadbury report on corporate governance provoked a wide range of reactions. On the one hand, there were those who complained that the report failed to go far enough to tackle the perceived problems of the abuse of power in listed companies, particularly those dominated by strong chairmen and CEOs. The report lacked teeth, it was argued. The code was voluntary, lacking legislative sanctions, with the ultimate threat of delisting from the stock exchange likely to harm shareholders, the very people Cadbury was supposed to be protecting. On the other hand, there was a vehement lobby which believed that the proposals – for the separation of chairman from CEO, powerful audit committees and independent directors with their own leader if necessary – were an attack on the very notion of the unitary board, introducing the suspect continental European two-tier board by the back door.

...and brought about changes

Given these two dramatically contrasting views,

Cadbury probably got it about right: certainly for starters. The significant effects that the report has had in the UK are now becoming clear, including changed attitudes towards board-level professionalism, wider disclosure on governance matters and in the continuing debate on governance.

The effect has been felt beyond the UK. In Canada, Malaysia, the Netherlands, Singapore, South Africa and other countries issues raised by Cadbury have been debated. In Australia Cadbury was influential in prompting a major reappraisal of governance, culminating in the Hilmer Report which took a different line from Cadbury. It argued that, although concern with shareholder protection was an important part of the board's duty, its key role was to ensure that corporate management was continuously and effectively striving for above-average performance, taking account of risk. In Hong Kong a direct result was a new requirement that all listed companies should have two independent non-executive directors. This may not appear dramatic, but it will change the balance of governance power, given that the Hong Kong Stock Exchange board has only one company that is truly in the hands of the public, the remainder being controlled to greater or lesser extent by dominant owners, particularly overseas Chinese family-based firms.

Adapting for the future

Corporate governance entails far more than financial control. It is about the exercise of power over the most influential entities in modern society. Future developments of corporate governance need to go way beyond discussions of board structures and governance mechanisms to focus on the reality of corporate power. What really happens at board level? What should happen? How is strategy formulated? Should the board set the corporate direction? Who supervises executive performance? To whom is the company and its board accountable? To whom should it be? The exercise of power (governance) over companies in the 21st century will depend on the answers to these questions.

Part 2
A–Z

A SHARE
See DIFFERENT TYPES OF SHARES.

ABI
See ASSOCIATION OF BRITISH INSURERS.

ACCOUNTABILITY
The directors of a company are primarily accountable to the shareholders. Such accountability is normally achieved through the regular DIRECTORS' REPORT AND ACCOUNTS and the ANNUAL GENERAL MEETING of the members (that is of the EQUITY shareholders) of the company. In most jurisdictions, however, there has been a tendency to call for wider accountability from boards, particularly in a PUBLIC COMPANY. Regulators demand wider disclosure of financial and other information. Employees' representatives expect information on matters that could affect their interests. (In Germany, the Netherlands and Sweden employees have statutory rights to board-level accountability.) Customer and other interest groups call for greater transparency of company activities. STAKEHOLDER THEORY argues that public companies have a duty to be accountable to all interest groups which could be affected by the company's actions (including customers, distributors, employees, financial institutions and suppliers, as well as local, national and international public interests).

> *The future role of corporate governance must be focused on better communication with shareholders, rather than on increasing the responsibilities of non-executive directors and institutional shareholders to oversee corporate management.*
> *Accountancy*, London, May 1997

ADDED-VALUE CHAIN ANALYSIS
Every business exists within the added-value chain within its industry; for example, the farmer grows wheat, the miller turns it into flour, the transport company carries it to the baker where it

is baked, or to the supermarket where it is sold to the end-user. Similarly each company has an added-value chain as the product or service is prepared for delivery to the customer.

A business may be heavily integrated with an upstream supply division or downstream channels; or at the other end of the scale it might have outsourced all but a core competence. The shoe firm Reebok, for example, has hardly any manufacturing and no retailing outlets, just a highly profitable managerial and marketing function. Analysing the elements of the added-value chain in a business can provide valuable strategic insights. Figure 10 illustrates a value-chain analysis for an electricity supply company.

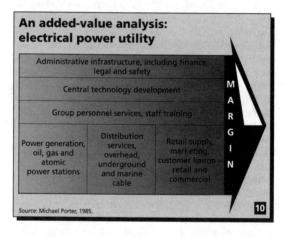

An added-value analysis: electrical power utility

Administrative infrastructure, including finance, legal and safety	M A R G I N
Central technology development	
Group personnel services, staff training	
Power generation, oil, gas and atomic power stations	Distribution services, overhead, underground and marine cable	Retail supply, marketing, customer liaison – retail and commercial	

Source: Michael Porter, 1985.

Each of the boxes in Figure 10 can be exploded into a whole set or hierarchy of more detailed diagrams that show just where value is being added. If associated with the related costs, a value-chain analysis will highlight which elements are driving costs and which are adding value. This information can be very important in STRATEGY FORMULATION because it can pinpoint the CORE COMPETENCES of the company and show how its activities are differentiated from those of alternative sources of supply. It can suggest new strategic options – both for improving existing activities and for developing new strategies such as outsourcing, backwards or forwards integration by acquisition, mergers or STRATEGIC ALLIANCES with firms offering similar services to obtain scale economies – share risk and enhance development.

ADJOURNMENT OF MEETINGS
See MEETING MANIPULATION.

ADVISORY BOARD
A non-statutory committee, typically without executive power, formed in various parts of the world by companies operating internationally, to give advice to the corporate directors and other decision-makers. Prominent business leaders, politicians and other influential figures from that region are usually invited to serve. Advisory boards were more prevalent in the 1970s and early 1980s. Companies have since found that the advice they need can be obtained more cheaply from consultants and commentators who can be retained only for as long as their advice is required. Some also found that advisory boards, although they had no formal executive authority, could create complications by making policy recommendations that were inconsistent with group-wide needs. For example, the advisory board might recommend investment in a given country, when the board's global strategy called for disinvestment there.

---

*Isn't it time we promoted young George
to the board?
But Mr George is 62.
Is he really? How well I remember his father.*

AGE OF DIRECTORS
An OUTSIDE DIRECTOR or NON-EXECUTIVE DIRECTOR tends to be older than an EXECUTIVE DIRECTOR. Three factors can restrict the age of directors: company law, which typically requires directors to be under 70 unless the shareholders have duly ap-

proved an exception; the company's own ARTICLES OF ASSOCIATION; and, for listed companies, the LISTING RULES of the relevant stock exchange.

AGENCY THEORY

A statistically powerful, theoretical base that can be used for gaining insights into the effect of a company's board on the performance of the business. The theory, as described by Jensen and Meckling in the *Journal of Financial Economics* in 1976, sees the relationship between directors and shareholders as:

> *A contract under which one or more persons (the principals) engage another person (the agent) to perform some service on their behalf which includes delegating some decision-making authority to the agent. If both parties to the relationship are utility maximisers there is good reason to believe the agent will not always act in the best interests of the principal.*

Exponents of agency theory quote examples of directors who have failed to act in the interests of the shareholders, treating the company as though it was their private fiefdom. Much research, using agency theory methods, has been published on board-level activities. Frequently these studies have attempted to show relationships between aspects of governance, such as board structure, DUALITY or directors' rewards, and overall corporate performance. But much of this work has been based on published data, such as the annual financial performance and board structures, and, furthermore, it has often been done by young researchers who have never met a company director.

As with some other powerful theories, agency theory provides a wonderfully (over) simple explanation of an aspect of economic life. Reality, unfortunately, is more complicated. Board behaviour does not consist exclusively of individual contractual relationships, but is influenced by interpersonal behaviour, group dynamics and political intrigue. Nor do all directors act in a way that makes the most of their personal interests: they can act responsibly with independence and integrity, as envisaged by the alternative STEWARD-SHIP THEORY. Nevertheless, insights from the research can challenge the shibboleths of conventional wisdom about the way boards work.

> *Statistical methods will not explain the reality of the boardroom.*
> Ada Demb, 1993

AGENDA

The order in which items are to be covered in a meeting. There are three approaches to agenda design.

1 The routine approach, in which each meeting follows the pattern of the previous one: apologies, approval of the MINUTES, matters arising, the usual substantive items and any other business.

2 The chairman-led approach, in which the chairman determines the agenda. Sir Norman Chester, who became warden of Nuffield College, Oxford, after a career in the British civil service, believed that good chairmen, among whom he counted himself, should put much effort into designing agenda. He recommended that care should be taken in selecting the items to be discussed, the time that should be allocated to each and their positioning on the agenda. Matters likely to be controversial should come towards the end, when members were expecting the meeting to end or had already left, thus increasing the chairman's chances of getting the decision he wants. He also believed in drafting the minutes along with the agenda, because those who draft the minutes – as every ambitious civil servant knows – can make them reflect their point of view.

3 The professional chairman approach, in which the chairman seeks advice on the agenda, perhaps from the COMPANY SECRETARY, or by asking each director whether there are items they wish to see discussed. Lord Caldecote, when chairman of the Delta Group, wrote to each of his directors periodically to ask whether there were matters they felt that the board should be discussing for the future benefit of the firm.

AGM
See ANNUAL GENERAL MEETING.

AIMA
Short for Australian Investment Managers Association, a frequent source of SHAREHOLDER ACTIVISM in Australia. The AIMA advises its clients on issues and recommends PROXY VOTING actions. (See also ABI, NAPF and PIRC.)

ALLIANCE BUILDING
See GAMES DIRECTORS PLAY.

ALTERNATE DIRECTOR
The ARTICLES OF ASSOCIATION of some companies allow the board to nominate alternate directors. This can be useful if board members have to travel a lot or are based out of the country in which board meetings are usually held. When serving in the alternate capacity, the alternate director has all the rights to INFORMATION and all the duties and responsibilities of every other director.

ANNUAL GENERAL MEETING
A properly convened meeting of all the voting EQUITY shareholders of the company. The annual general meeting (AGM) is part of the formal machinery of CORPORATE GOVERNANCE, providing an opportunity for the directors to demonstrate their ACCOUNTABILITY to the owners. Certain decisions, such as the approval of the annual accounts and dividend, the appointment of directors and the confirmation of the auditors, are statutorily required to be taken by the AGM. The detailed rules, such as the amount of notice required and rules for voting (including proxy votes), are usually contained in the company's ARTICLES OF ASSOCIATION. Some jurisdictions allow small, closely held

companies to forgo their AGM, because all members can be presumed to know the company's affairs sufficiently well and to be able to exert their influence over them.

In the United States directors of listed companies expect to be extensively questioned at their AGMS. Indeed, they are often briefed, even rehearsed, on possible enquiries. In Japan the AGMS of all listed companies are nearly always held on the same day to prevent the disruption of the meeting by paid troublemakers from the *YAKUZA*. In the UK and most European countries, by contrast, AGMS have tended to be brief, formal, entirely predictable affairs in which any sign of critical questioning is thwarted from the chair and the only shareholder comment is a vote of thanks to the chairman and the board. Recently, however, there have been signs of an end to that complacency. Institutional and private investors have begun to demand answers to questions on matters such as DIRECTORS' REMUNERATION and the company's (and by implication its board's) performance.

AMAKADURI
See DESCENT FROM HEAVEN.

ARTICLES OF ASSOCIATION
The formal set of rules by which a company is run. Registered with the company regulatory authorities at the time of incorporation, in accordance with the company law in that jurisdiction, the articles provide an important element in the CORPORATE GOVERNANCE mechanisms. Articles can be amended by a resolution formally approved by a meeting of the company's members. Directors should always study the articles of a company on whose board they serve. Occasionally nonstandard drafting can have unexpected effects on director powers and board decisions. For example, an owner-manager of a company incorporated in the UK that was in a JOINT VENTURE with a Japanese SHAREHOLDER was thwarted in his attempt to bring in new capital. He believed he had control because he held 61% of the voting shares,

only to discover that to exercise such powers, the articles called for the approval of 75% of the shareholders.

ASIAN VALUES

One of the explanations offered to explain decades of economic success in certain East Asian countries: business and governance practices rooted in a strong work ethic, a commitment to saving and a family-centric culture. Following the financial and economic crisis that hit countries such as Indonesia, Malaysia, Thailand and South Korea in late 1997, CRONY CAPITALISM was offered as an alternative governance insight.

ASSOCIATE DIRECTOR

Some companies give the title of director to senior managers, even though they are not formally on the board. One reason might be to reward managerial performance with recognition and status; another might be to give prestige to an executive who is required to represent the company with clients, customers or government. Even though they have not been appointed by the shareholders, nor recognised as directors by the filing requirements of companies' acts and stock exchange listing agreements, such people could find themselves held responsible like other directors if those with whom they had dealt reasonably thought they were directors. (See also TITLES.)

ASSOCIATION OF BRITISH INSURERS

An organisation representing the interests of INSTITUTIONAL INVESTORS among British insurance companies. The Association of British Insurers (ABI) has taken a higher profile in CORPORATE GOVERNANCE issues in recent years, monitoring company activities against codes of good corporate governance conduct, occasionally advising on SHAREHOLDER ACTIVISM and PROXY VOTING options. (See also NATIONAL ASSOCIATION OF PENSION FUNDS.)

AUDIT

In most jurisdictions companies are required to

have an audit so that the auditors can report to the shareholders that the annual report and accounts presented to them by the directors show a true and fair view of the state of the company's affairs, although the exact wording varies. In some jurisdictions quarterly accounts also have to be audited; in others closely held private companies may dispense with the audit, if the shareholders agree; and in a few, such as the British Virgin Islands, there is no audit requirement at all.

Audit committees will fall short of their potential if they lack the understanding to deal adequately with the auditing or accounting matters that they are likely to face.
Cadbury Report, 1992

Experience has shown that audit committees have developed into essential committees of boards of directors.
European Commission Report, 1996 Green Paper on Auditing

AUDIT COMMITTEE

The relationship with the external, independent auditors is crucial to board-level effectiveness. All directors need to know what issues have arisen during the AUDIT. The board must avoid the possibility of a powerful executive director, such as the finance director or the CEO, dominating the relationship with the AUDITOR, resolving all matters before they reach the board. An audit committee can avoid such problems. A subcommittee of the main board, the audit committee is made up wholly, or with a majority, of outside directors. Its role is to act as a bridge between the external auditors and the board. Typically audit committees meet three or four times a year to discuss the details of the audit, to consider any contentious points that have arisen in the accounts and to receive the auditor's recommendations on audit matters such as management controls.

The audit committee will also usually be concerned with the appointment of auditors and the negotiation of the audit fee. Problems can arise if an audit committee goes beyond its bridging role with the auditors and begins to interfere in management's legitimate responsibilities. The New York Stock Exchange requires an audit committee as a condition of listing. In the UK the Cadbury Committee on the financial aspects of CORPORATE GOVERNANCE recommended an audit committee for all UK listed companies in its code of best practice. This requirement has now been incorporated into the London Stock Exchange's listing requirements. (See Appendix 4.)

Even though it is primarily the responsibility of directors, auditors cannot avoid responsibility for ensuring good corporate governance and for taking action, privately or publicly. The public expect it.

Christopher Pearce, chairman,
The 100 Group of Finance Directors, UK

Auditors are like the cuckoos in cuckoo clocks: they come out, comment briefly and nip back inside. Ticking is what they do best.

Robert Hodgkinson, chairman,
Financial Reporting Council, London

AUDITOR

Independent outside auditors fulfil a crucial role in CORPORATE GOVERNANCE. Usually appointed formally by the members, on the recommendation of the incumbent board, the auditors report on the directors' report and accounts submitted to the members by the board. Should the AUDIT throw up disagreements that cannot be reconciled with the company's directors, the auditor will qualify the audit report. In recent years auditors of major public companies around the world have found themselves the subject of LITIGATION from dissatisfied shareholders and others when subsequent events raise questions about the validity of audited financial statements. This can be caused by the DEEP POCKET SYNDROME. To ensure that the find-

---

ings of the auditors are available to the entire board, including any outside directors, conventional wisdom now recommends the creation of an AUDIT COMMITTEE.

AUFSICHTSRAT

The upper SUPERVISORY BOARD of the German form of TWO-TIER BOARD. Large companies in Germany are seen as a form of "partnership" between capital and labour. Reflecting this approach to worker co-determination, the *Aufsichtsrat* has half its members representing the shareholders and half the employees.

B

B SHARE

Each EQUITY share normally carries one vote; indeed "one share, one vote" has been a cause pursued by some advocates of SHAREHOLDER democracy. Occasionally, however, dominant owner-managers in public companies find the need for additional funding from the public, but realise that issuing more shares will dilute their holdings below the point at which they can maintain control. A way round this is to issue some B shares carrying a disproportionately large number of votes (perhaps 100) per share. In this way the additional equity shares will not dilute their voting capacity below the controlling level.

A good example of the use of B shares is the activities of the late Dr An Wang, who built up Wang Laboratories dramatically during the 1970s and early 1980s. Though highly successful at that time, ploughing back profits was not enough to fund the additional capital needs of the rapidly expanding company. But raising more capital on the market would have diluted the voting power of the shares owned by the founder below that needed to maintain control. Like other Chinese entrepreneurs, Dr Wang wanted to keep control within the family. Wang Laboratories was listed on the New York Stock Exchange, which at that time did not allow the DUAL CLASS SHARE. So Dr Wang re-listed the shares on the smaller American Stock Exchange. He was advised that the share price might suffer because investors would view the shares as more risky, with the company dominated by him and his family interests. In the event the share price increased following the re-listing with B shares. For a while the company continued to prosper, but it eventually failed to adapt to strategic changes in its markets and family control was lost.

BOARD EFFECTIVENESS

There was a time when a director had to do little more than attend an occasional meeting, make a few personal observations and look forward to receiving a fee. But that was in the days when people rode to meetings on a horse. Today shareholders, regulators and other stakeholders have high expectations of directors. Requirements from regulators continue to grow, pressures from institutional investors have become significant, and there is an increasing threat of LITIGATION against the company, the board and individual directors for malpractice or negligence. Under such circumstances the need for board-level effectiveness has never been higher. In response some boards are now specifically considering the CORE COMPETENCES that are needed in directors, systematically reviewing the performance of the board, and developing strategies for board-level development. (See the MTRC case study in Appendix 2.)

Once on the board, directors seem to stay for ever. I would like to see a "sell-by" date stamped on the head of every director.
David Norburn, Chicago, 1993

BOARD GUIDELINES
Few companies, including even the most significant around the world, have written board guidelines. General Motors is one exception. Its seemingly exhaustive guidelines for the board (see Appendix 3) include guidance on:

- the separation of chairman and CEO;
- the concept of LEAD DIRECTOR;
- the number of board committees;
- the assignment and rotation of committee members;
- the frequency and length of committee meetings;
- committee AGENDA;
- the selection of agenda items for board meetings;
- board materials distributed in advance;
- presentations to the directors;
- regular attendance of non-directors at board meetings;
- executive sessions of outside directors;

- board access to senior management;
- board compensation review;
- size of the board;
- mix of inside and outside directors;
- definition of independence for outside directors;
- former CEO's board membership;
- board membership criteria;
- selection of new directors;
- assessing the board's performance;
- directors who change their present job responsibilities;
- term limits;
- retirement age;
- evaluation of the CEO;
- board succession planning;
- top management development;
- board interaction with institutional investors, the press, customers and other stakeholders.

Other companies are now following suit.

The most important factor governing a successful board is the quality of the board itself ... Board meetings must not be solemn affairs ... There is no absolute magic formula. Every company has its own culture and metabolism, and different types of business require separate types of management style and approach from the board.
Sir Richard Greenbury, chairman of Marks & Spencer, UK

BOARD LIFE CYCLE

Businesses have a tendency to outgrow their boards. A successful contribution to the board in the past does not guarantee a continuing contribution in the future, if the strategic situation facing the company changes significantly. Yet few boards have formal director development and succession plans; even fewer have a strategy for board development that will ensure that the board changes in line with proposed changes in the overall corporate strategy.

BOARD MEETING

A board of directors can meet when and where it wants, subject to anything in the ARTICLES OF ASSO-CIATION. Some boards have few meetings, either because the directors meet regularly on an informal basis, so that the board meetings become an occasion for formalising decisions taken, or because the activities of the company do not require more meetings. Professional boards, however, usually have a regular schedule of meetings (often monthly). (See also BOARD STYLE.)

Boards have an unlimited capacity for self-delusion. The way they work is a black box.
Andrew Pettigrew, Warwick Business School, November 1997

BOARD STRUCTURE

The UNITARY BOARD, unlike the TWO-TIER BOARD, is the sole governing body in many company law jurisdictions. Typically, the unitary board includes both executive and outside non-executive directors. In many small and family firms the board is entirely executive; others have a minority non-executive membership. Yet others, including the majority of public companies in Australia and the United States, have a majority of outside directors. A few companies, particularly in the non-profit sector, have an entirely non-executive board, with the chief executive and possibly other top executives in attendance. The minimum and maximum size of a board may be constrained by the ARTICLES OF ASSOCIATION, which may be amended with the formal approval of the shareholders.

The Board of IBM in the late 1980s was far too large, with 18 members, to be an effective committee. It was headed by a chairman who was also the chief executive; it was stuffed with retirees (a third of the number, including the former chairman); and it was short on relevant business experience. Eight members were drafted from other industries. None of their companies manufactured or marketed in ways remotely

*analogous to IBM's processes and procedures and
needs. The others included a lawyer, three
academics and the former secretary for defence.
Few held any significant ownership stake in IBM.
This type of boardroom construction works well
for a company that is running well and is led by
an executive team which knows where it is going
and why. In cases like IBM during the crisis
years, more was required of the outside directors
than they could provide in terms of relevant and
current business experience and skills.*

Wong Kai Wa, Aaron: the perspective of an MBA student

*Boards should play greater attention to the
calibre as well as the mix of directors, recognising
that effective board membership requires high
levels of intellectual ability, experience, soundness
of judgment and integrity.*

The Hilmer Report, *Strictly Boardroom*, Australia 1993

BOARD STYLE

Boards can vary dramatically in their approach to
their work. Some have a rather comfortable,
COUNTRY CLUB BOARD style, others may act as a
RUBBER STAMP for management proposals. Some are
REPRESENTATIVE BOARDS with directors representing
various interest groups and are consequently
more political in style, while others adopt a professional approach with a concern for both the
strategic direction of the company and the supervision of executive performance.

*What matters is not only the structure of
boards but how they work.*

Sir Adrian Cadbury, speaking in Australia, 1993

*... there was no attempt to make management
accountable to anyone. On the contrary boards
of directors – legally the governing body of the
corporation – became increasingly impotent
rubber stamps for a company's top management.*

Peter Drucker, *Post-capitalist Society*, 1993

*To my way of thinking the General Motors board
has a unique function of great significance. That
is what I call an "audit function". I do not mean
audit in the usual financial sense but one that
contemplates a continuous review and appraisal
of what is going on throughout the enterprise.
It is impossible to conceive of every member of
the corporation's board of directors having
intimate knowledge of, and business experience
in, every one of the technical matters which
require top level consideration or action.
Nevertheless, the board can and should be
responsible for the end result.*
Alfred P. Sloan, *My Years with General Motors*, 1963

*The words of Mr Sloan take on a new
significance: "I happen to be one of the old school
who thinks that a knowledge of the business is
essential to a successful organisation." That is
simply not the case today at General Motors.*
John de Lorean,
On a Clear Day You Can See General Motors, 1979
(Of course this was long before General Motors introduced
the Board Guidelines that are reproduced in Appendix 3.)

BOESKY, IVAN

A securities dealer in the United States who epito-
mised the money and growth culture of the 1980s.
A colleague of Dennis LEVINE, Ivan Boesky told a
business school graduation ceremony at the University of California: "I want you to know that I
think that greed is healthy. It is the basis of the
capitalist system." He received rapturous ap-
plause; such was the business climate in the mid-
1980s. Subsequently, he went to jail on INSIDER
DEALING charges.

BUDGETARY PLANNING

An approach to STRATEGY FORMULATION. If entrepreneurial strategies developed by the founder of
a business seem to be failing, the other directors
may try to superimpose order. Often they call for
more formal planning, more control of acquisi-

tions and investment decisions and less reactive deal-making. Budgetary planning and control is emphasised, so that the board can approve spending plans and be more closely involved in monitoring performance. More managers within the organisation now participate in the planning process, forecasting anticipated levels of activity, planned revenues, costs and profits. Such planning is often tied to formal accounting processes and annual budgets and is financially oriented, relatively short-term and based on internal organisational units such as cost and profit centres.

Critics of accountancy-based planning systems argue that they cannot be truly strategic because they are short-term, linked to annual accounting cycles and do not reflect the natural strategic time horizons of the business. Proponents of financially based planning suggest that this problem can be overcome by long-range planning, in which forecasts are projected further forward and budget plans extended for longer periods, perhaps three to five years. If competition and markets were predictable and slow to change, this might be feasible. In most of today's globally influenced markets it is not.

Two other criticisms of financially oriented corporate planning are that it undervalues other vital factors, such as product and market strategies, and it is company centred. The strategist is inside the company looking out, whereas HELICOPTER VISION is needed, that is looking down at the company in its industry and market context.

BULLOCK REPORT
Sir Alan Bullock (now Lord Bullock), when master of St Catherine's College, Oxford, was asked in 1976 by the British prime minister, Harold Wilson, to chair an inquiry into industrial democracy. This was a response to the European Community's proposals, in the fifth draft directive on company law harmonisation, that major companies in all EC countries should adopt the German TWO-TIER BOARD structure in which half the members of the SUPERVISORY BOARD represented capital (elected by

the shareholders) and the other half represented employees (elected through trade union representation). The Bullock Report recommended the continuation of the British type of UNITARY BOARD, but it did suggest that a proportion of the directors be elected, through trade union machinery, to represent employee concerns. Business interests were highly critical of both the Bullock proposals and the draft fifth directive. Neither has been enacted.

CADBURY REPORT

Prominent institutions in the City of London, concerned about AUDIT and regulatory issues following a number of dramatic company collapses in the 1980s, set up a committee chaired by Sir Adrian Cadbury. To avoid the potential domination of companies by over-powerful chief executives or over-enthusiastic executive management, the committee's 1992 report entitled "The Financial Aspects of Corporate Governance" advocated the following checks and balances at board level:

- wider use of independent non-executive directors;
- the introduction of an AUDIT COMMITTEE;
- a separation between chairman and CEO;
- the use of a REMUNERATION COMMITTEE;
- adherence to a detailed code of best practice.

Under the code all UK listed companies were required to report to shareholders on their governance practices, with the ultimate threat of delisting for non-compliance.

Reactions to the Cadbury Report varied. Some argued that it lacked teeth, claiming that delisting, being the ultimate sanction, would disadvantage the very shareholders who the report set out to protect, and that nothing short of legislation would stop abuses by dominant company leaders. Others feared that giving non-executives more power (Cadbury recommended that they appoint their own leader, have access to legal advice and meet separately if necessary) would erode the concept of the UNITARY BOARD, creating the continental European TWO-TIER BOARD by the back door. In the event most listed companies decided to comply with the code of best practice, except in the requirement to create a NOMINATING COMMITTEE of independent outside directors to recommend names for board appointment.

CALPERS

The Californian State Employees Pension Fund

(CALPERS) has been the most proactive institutional investor in the United States, setting a trend in SHAREHOLDER ACTIVISM throughout the country. Now its attention has turned to CORPORATE GOVERNANCE in the international arena. It published a set of global principles for corporate governance in December 1996: "All markets should develop an appropriate code of best practice, by which directors can regulate themselves ... Such a code should be representative of the best governance practice in the market."

The lesson from the Cadbury Report is that greater disclosure is starting to force more careful consideration by the board of company performance, internal management and financial control issues, the setting of strategic goals and companies' competitive positions.
Accountancy, London, May 1997

CATALYST
One role a director can play (see CONFORMANCE ROLES).

CECIL KING CLAUSE
Acting in line with the company's ARTICLES OF ASSOCIATION, in 1968 the board of the International Publishing Corporation removed their chairman, Cecil King. Since then such provisions in company's articles have been called Cecil King clauses. Many company articles now include such clauses, sometimes requiring unanimity from the other board members and sometimes not. Despite such provisions, some argue that it is still difficult to remove an under-performing director. To achieve the necessary support a director has to declare his position, which may well put his own tenure in jeopardy.

CHAEBOL
Large conglomerate groups of companies in South Korea, dominated by family interests, formed after the second world war with close government involvement. Recently the government has sought

to reduce the power of the *chaebol* by requiring them to divest some of their interests. It had little success before the financial and economic crisis of late 1997. Now such changes are being forced on some *chaebol* by economic conditions. Unable to cut costs because of a tradition of life-time employment and militant trade unions, the *chaebol* are finding it difficult to compete with other Asian producers.

The role of chairman circa AD 400:
The Abbot shall call together the whole congregation of the brethren to take council. He shall himself explain the questions at issue. And having had the advice of the brethren, he shall think it over himself, and shall do what he considers most advantageous.
Saint Benedict, *Rules for Monks*

CHAIR

Many people speak loosely of the chairman of the company, whereas his or her role is, strictly, that of chairman of the company's board of directors. Subject to anything in the company's ARTICLES OF ASSOCIATION, the directors appoint one of their number to take the chair at their meetings. There are few statutory requirements for the role so a range of styles is to be found. At one extreme the chairman does no more than manage the meetings, arrange the AGENDA, steer the discussions and ensure that they reach a conclusion. At the other extreme is the powerful chairman who acts as a figurehead for the company, influences its strategic direction and manages the board, being concerned with its membership, committees and overall performance as well as chairing board meetings.

There has been much debate about DUALITY, that is whether the role of chairman and CEO should be separate or combined. The CADBURY REPORT recommended that they should be separate; but if they were combined then the role of the independent NON-EXECUTIVE DIRECTOR should be enhanced. In Australia the roles have for many years generally been separate. In the UK they have become increasingly separate, although a number of dominant individuals, in total command of their companies, continue to hold both titles. In the United States the predominant practice has been to combine the roles, but in the context of boards which have a majority of outside directors. However, there are now calls from INSTITUTIONAL INVESTORS for a separation of the roles in US companies.

The era of political correctness has caused many organisations to reconsider the title of the chairman of their governing body and its committees. Lady chairman, chairwoman, or even the name of a piece of furniture, the chair, are used. Worldwide the number of women chairing the boards of major companies is minimal. But in many charitable and other non-profit companies women play a significant board role.

I am pleased to see the demise of "chairperson" which has a deathly ring of political correctness. I'm not keen on "chair". The best choice is chairman which, like manhole, does not require feminising. However, those who enjoy gallant gestures might like to use the elegant epithet "Madam Chairman".

John Morgan, writing on modern manners
in *The Times*, London 1998

CHINESE CORPORATE GOVERNANCE

China is providing the rest of the world with a laboratory for CORPORATE GOVERNANCE thinking. In a country influenced by Marxist thinking, OWNERSHIP is not the basis of power. But, as the country adapts to the ways of the market, advice on securities regulation, accounting standards and corporate governance is being sought and readily given by institutions and individuals from Hong Kong, the UK and the United States.

At present, the few Chinese companies that

have come to the market outside China seem to be strongly influenced by their top management. Their boards have to cope with multiple calls for control from various authorities – the relevant industry ministry in Beijing, the People's Bank of China, tax and regulatory bodies, and state, provincial and industry officials – who are concerned to avoid both unacceptable economic and social stresses such as unemployment, bankruptcy, corruption, financial pressures on the state economy and undesirable competition with state enterprises. A form of SUPERVISORY BOARD structure has been adopted, with outside members including Communist Party officials such as the local party secretary. Although their powers are in the process of definition, it appears that these may be more political and exhortatory, rather than the explicit "hire and fire" power over the executive board enjoyed by the European TWO-TIER BOARD.

Power will probably reside with top management and officialdom. The notion of independent outside directors does not seem to be a remedy for SHAREHOLDER protection, because of the lack of those with the necessary experience and power. Disclosure and accountability rules seem to offer the best hope, with the notion of a shareholders' committee to represent the interests of both international B SHARE and local A share investors.

Overseas capital is available for companies incorporated in China through two routes. The first involves a listing of the Chinese business on an overseas stock market. To date this has mainly been in Hong Kong, although companies have been listed in Australia and the United States. In Hong Kong some Chinese companies have been listed in their own right, going through the same due diligence and prospectus requirements as other companies. Others have listed through the back door by acquiring a company that already has a listing and using this as a SHELL COMPANY into which the China business is incorporated. Of course, all companies have to abide by the listing regulations of the Hong Kong stock exchange and the auditing and governance requirements of the Companies Ordinance. The second route is to issue B shares in China, available only to foreigners, on either the Shenzen (the special economic zone on Hong Kong's northern border) or the Shanghai stock exchanges.

CIRCUIT BREAKER

After the 1987 stockmarket crash, trading breaks were instituted by various stock exchanges. These are points at which trading would be suspended should the market fall a certain distance (350 and 550 points on the New York Stock Exchange) to give time for reflection, avoid panic selling and prevent prices going into free-fall. Subsequent experience has led to alternative forms of triggering the circuit breaker being proposed, such as when the market falls a certain percentage.

CLOSELY HELD COMPANY

A PRIVATE COMPANY in which the shareholders and directors are effectively the same people. Consequently, many of the CORPORATE GOVERNANCE checks and balances that are needed to protect the rights of the SHAREHOLDER, where there is a separation between OWNERSHIP and management, are unnecessary. In some jurisdictions such companies are exempt from some AUDIT, disclosure and filing requirements. (See FAMILY DIRECTOR.)

COALITION BUILDING

See GAMES DIRECTORS PLAY.

COMPANY LIMITED BY GUARANTEE

A type of CORPORATE ENTITY in which the guarantors agree to subscribe, to the extent of the guarantee given on incorporation, should the company be wound up. By contrast, in the JOINT STOCK LIMITED LIABILITY COMPANY a SHAREHOLDER's liability is limited to the extent of its EQUITY stake. Companies limited by guarantee are often incorporated to limit the liability of members of non-profit organisations such as academic and

educational bodies, cultural and sports organisations or welfare and other charitable bodies.
These companies need boards and directors,
however, and most of the material in this book
will be relevant to them.

COMPANY SECRETARY

An officer of the company who can, potentially,
make an important contribution to the board. As
the CADBURY REPORT suggested:

> *The company secretary has a key role to play
> in ensuring that board procedures are both
> followed and regularly reviewed. The
> chairman and the board will look to the
> company secretary for guidance on what their
> responsibilities are under the rules and
> regulations to which they are subject and on
> how those responsibilities should be
> discharged. All directors should have access to
> the advice and services of the company
> secretary and should recognise that the
> chairman is entitled to the strong support of
> the company secretary in ensuring the
> effective functioning of the board.*

In the United States the company secretary is
known as the corporate secretary. The American
Society of Corporate Secretaries suggests that their
duties and responsibilities include organising
meetings of the board, board committees and
shareholders, maintaining the corporate records
and stock (SHAREHOLDER) records and liaising with
the securities markets. It further states that the
company secretary should be "the primary liaison
between the corporation's directors and management". The company secretary need not be an
employee of the company; he or she may work
for an outside agency or partnership. In some
jurisdictions the function can be fulfilled by another corporation. In other countries, including
Australia, the company secretary must be a
natural person.

The evolution of the company secretary's role

reflects how much corporate life has changed. When the JOINT STOCK LIMITED LIABILITY COMPANY was developed in the UK in the mid-19th century, the directors needed someone to keep their records. This was the job of the secretary to the board. The function was largely clerical, with the directors holding the power.

Changing attitudes to company secretaries can be seen in the contrasting comments of two senior British judges. In 1887 Lord Esher, Master of the Rolls, said:

> *A secretary is a mere servant. His position is that he is to do what he is told and no person can assume that he has the authority to represent anything at all, nor can anyone assume that statements made by him are necessarily accepted as trustworthy without further enquiry.*

A hundred years later things had changed. Corporate life has become complicated. Many companies run diverse enterprises through complex groups of subsidiary and associated companies. Legislation affecting companies has become substantial. Now the role of the company secretary calls for professional knowledge and skill. In 1971 Lord Denning, Master of the Rolls, said:

> *Times have changed. A company secretary is a much more important person nowadays than he was in 1871. He is an officer of the company with extensive duties and responsibilities. This appears not only in modern Companies Acts but also in the role which he plays in the day-to-day business of companies. He is no longer merely a clerk. He regularly makes representations on behalf of the company and enters into contracts on its behalf ... so much so that he may be regarded as held out to do such things on behalf of the company. He is certainly entitled to sign contracts connected with the administrative side of the company's affairs, such as*

*employing staff, ordering cars and so forth.
All such matters come within the ostensible
authority of a company secretary.*

CONFIDANTE

One of the roles a director can play (see CONFORM-
ANCE ROLES).

CONFORMANCE ROLES

There are two principal sets of roles that every
UNITARY BOARD of directors and governing body
must fulfil: conformance roles and PERFORMANCE
ROLES. The conformance roles involve EXECUTIVE
SUPERVISION and ACCOUNTABILITY. In recent years
many of the developments in corporate regulation
around the world, such as the CADBURY REPORT,
have emphasised the conformance role of boards.

The main conformance roles of directors are as
follows.

Judge Directors playing this role are able to
make an objective assessment of a situation. This
can be a vital contribution of outside directors,
who have the opportunity to see board matters
from an external and independent point of view.
Such an objective evaluation of top management
performance can overcome the tunnel vision
sometimes found in those too closely involved
with the situation, or the myopia brought on by
being personally affected by the outcome.

Catalyst This role is played by directors who
are capable of questioning the board's assumptions and causing change in others' thinking. Catalysts point out that what appears to be an
incontrovertible truth to some board members is,
in fact, rooted in questionable beliefs that others
have about the company, its markets, its competitors and so on. They highlight inferences that are
masquerading as facts and indicate when value
judgments, rather than rigorous analysis, are being
used in board deliberations. Most valuably, catalysts stimulate the board discussions with new,
alternative insights and ideas.

Supervisor It is the role of the whole board to

monitor and supervise executive management. But the calls for non-executive directors, for a separation of the chairmanship from the chief executive responsibility and for the use of audit, nominating and remuneration committees emphasise the value of the supervisor role of outside directors.

Watch dog Directors who cast themselves in this role see themselves as the protector of the interests of other parties, such as the shareholders or, more often, a specific interest group. Representative or nominee directors inevitably find themselves in this position, as they look out for the interests of the party that put them on the board. This might be a major investor for a director on the board of an American or British listed company, the employees for a director on a German SUPERVISORY BOARD, or the KEIRETSU group interests for a director on the board of a major Japanese company. Every director has a duty to be concerned with the interests of the company as a whole (that is with the interests of all the members without discrimination), so the watch-dog role has to be applied with care.

Confidante Some directors may find themselves acting as a sounding board for other directors, the chief executive or the chairman; a trusted and respected counsellor in times of uncertainty and stress; someone to share concerns with about issues (often interpersonal problems) outside the boardroom. Political process at board level inevitably involves the use, and sometimes abuse, of power. The confidante can make a valuable contribution. But it is vital that he or she commands the trust of all the directors, otherwise the problem may be reinforced rather than resolved.

Safety valve It is legitimate for directors to act as safety valves at a time of crisis, in order to release the pressure, prevent further damage and save the situation. A classic example would be when the company has run into financial problems, management performance has deteriorated and the chief executive has to be replaced. Another example might be if the company faced an unexpected catastrophe. The sensible and steadying counsel of a wise member of the board can save an otherwise disastrous situation.

CONTACT PERSON
One of the roles a director can play (see PERFORMANCE ROLES).

CORE CAPABILITIES
See CORE COMPETENCES.

CORE COMPETENCES
The hidden strengths of a business that the directors can call on during STRATEGY FORMULATION. Unlike the more obvious resources that a company has, such as its product portfolio, its financial position and its organisational characteristics, core competences reflect the knowledge in the organisation and its learning capability. A core competence in a financial institution might be its strength in handling derivatives, in a software house its experience in networking applications, or in an automobile manufacturer its knowledge of electronic controls. Some refer to core competences as core capabilities, broadening the definition to include, for example, the ability of an entertainment company to deliver its video product over cable television, or of a retail chain store to access its suppliers directly by satellite-based electronic data interchange.

Strategic thinking in Western companies in recent years has emphasised the benefits of identifying the core competences and capabilities of the firm and building on them to the exclusion of all else. This includes not only the divesting of conglomerate businesses, unrelated to the core activities, but also outsourcing other functions so that both financial and managerial resources can be concentrated on the activities that are crucial to the company's strategic performance. Asian companies, by and large, do not share this enthusiasm for concentration, seeing business more as a series of trading opportunities which enable transient networks of inter-trading entities to be created, often with cross-holdings and cross-directorships.

CORE VALUES

A statement, typically approved at board level, of the underlying beliefs that a company has about itself and its relations with those involved with it. The core values of a passenger transport company, for example, might include statements that it is dedicated to safety, customer service and cost-effective travel, while providing rewarding career opportunities and job satisfaction for its staff, and a reasonable reward for its investors. The articulation of core values can influence the process of STRATEGY FORMULATION and POLICY-MAKING, not least because it tends to define the playing field, the games that are to be played and the rules by which the company intends to operate. (See also MISSION STATEMENT.)

All hail astonishing fact,
All hail invention new,
The joint stock company act,
of parliament, sixty two.
And soon or late I always call
for Stock Exchange quotation,
No scheme too great, and none too small
for companification.
Gilbert and Sullivan, Utopia Ltd

In the three years 1845–1847, at the height of the railway mania in the UK, 425 new railway companies were incorporated in Britain, with a total proposed capital of over £213 million. This was equal to two thirds of all exports for 1846. The share capital of the Bank of England at the time was £16.6 million.
Adrian Vaughan, *Railwaymen, Politics and Money*, 1997

CORPORATE ENTITY

The development of the corporate concept in the middle of the 19th century enabled massive capital formation, dramatic industrial development and untold wealth creation around the world. Previously, the only way to organise business was as a sole trader or partnership, in which, if the business failed, the debtor went to prison and his family to the poor-house. The JOINT STOCK LIMITED LIABILITY COMPANY enabled a legal entity to be incorporated with an existence separate from its owners, whose liability for the company's debts was limited to their equity stake. Such a corporate entity can contract, sue and be sued independently of those who have provided the capital. A dramatically simple and superbly successful concept originally, the notion of corporate entity has now become complex, with many different types of corporate structures, many forms of financial instruments and complicated international corporate networks.

CORPORATE GOVERNANCE

The way power is exercised over a CORPORATE ENTITY and the overall subject of this book. All corporate entities need to be governed as well as managed. The structure and processes of the governing body, typically the board of directors in a JOINT STOCK LIMITED LIABILITY COMPANY, is central to corporate governance. The relationships between the board and the shareholders, the auditors, the regulators and other stakeholders is also crucial to effective corporate governance, as is the linkage between the board and top management. Corporate governance is a relatively new field of study. The first book with the title *Corporate Governance* was published in 1984 and the academic journal *Corporate Governance – an international review* was launched in 1993.

Effective corporate governance ensures that long-term strategic objectives and plans are established and that the proper management and management structure are in place to achieve those objectives, while at the same time making sure that the structure functions to maintain the corporation's integrity, reputation and accountability to its constituencies.
The National Association of Corporate Directors, Washington, US

A key question currently confronting the Congress is whether something is so fundamentally wrong with the structure of corporate governance that it requires legislative remedy. In principle, corporations are run for the benefit of shareholders, within the context of laws that are designed to protect the rights of third parties. Such protections, whether for employees, the community or the environment, should not be obligations of corporate management. They are appropriately left to statute...

Alan Greenspan, *Wall Street Journal*, 1987

CORPORATE PLANNING

An analytical and professional approach to the board's PERFORMANCE ROLES. Growing competition around the world during the 1960s professionalised corporate planning. Firms could no longer sell all they could produce. A market-oriented professionalism began to emerge. Management consultants offered analytical tools such as PORTFOLIO ANALYSIS, PRODUCT MAPPING, SCENARIO BUILDING, SWOT ANALYSIS and VALUE-CHAIN ANALYSIS. Corporate planning departments were created. Directors were drawn into the strategic thinking process.

CORPORATE SENATE

An idea developed by Shann Turnbull in Australia. He has suggested that "most corporations in the English-speaking world are essentially corrupt because their UNITARY BOARD structures concentrate on conflicts of interest and corporate power". His alternative is a dual board structure with a corporate senate with not more than three members, elected on the basis of one vote per SHAREHOLDER, not per share. The senate would have no proactive power but the right to veto where it feels the board has a conflict of interest. Modelled on the successful Spanish Mondragon worker co-operatives, Mr Turnbull has applied the concept to public companies he has formed.

CORPORATE SOCIAL RESPONSIBILITY
See ETHICS.

CORPORATE STRATEGY
See STRATEGY FORMULATION.

CORPORATE VEIL
A legal phrase emphasising that a company, incorporated with limited liability, is surrounded by a veil that creditors may not pierce to pursue payment of their debts from the SHAREHOLDER owners. In common law jurisdictions this even applies to subsidiary companies that are wholly owned by a parent company which controls their activities. In other words, the holding company may walk away from its subsidiary's debts. In some other jurisdictions, including Germany, creditors may pursue their debts up the corporate chain of dominating companies in a group, thus piercing the corporate veil.

CORPORATISATION
See PRIVATISATION.

COUNTRY CLUB BOARD
A BOARD STYLE in which directors pay more attention to their interpersonal relationships, board rituals and the board atmosphere, than they do to tough-minded, goal-oriented decision-making.

CRONY CAPITALISM
An insight into the exercise of CORPORATE GOVERNANCE power in certain countries in East Asia, offered to explain the economic shocks that hit the region in late 1997, where business had been facilitated by close links between directors and members of government, the ruling elite or business associates, rather than by sound business logic.

CRONYISM
See GAMES DIRECTORS PLAY.

CROSS-DIRECTORSHIP
See INTERLOCKING DIRECTORSHIP

CROSS-HOLDING
The holding of EQUITY voting shares by companies in each other. The practice is prevalent in Asia where many companies build networks of alliances and share risk. Cross-directorships are often found where there are cross-holdings of shares. Some jurisdictions prohibit a subsidiary company holding shares in its parent, thus reducing the potential of cross-holdings. (See also *KEIRETSU*.)

CROWN JEWELS
A takeover defence used by some boards of directors of potential target companies in which they contract with another party to license or acquire a right in significant company assets. The aim is to reduce the attractiveness of the company to predators. The terms of such an arrangement allow the other party to buy out the company at a predetermined price should the takeover materialise, or obtain damages in lieu.

D

D&O INSURANCE
See INDEMNITY INSURANCE.

DEEP-POCKET SYNDROME
When a company is in financial difficulty or has become insolvent, there may be little point in shareholders or creditors suing the company because it has no money. Instead, as has become increasingly the case, their best option has been to take legal actions against those who are covered by INDEMNITY INSURANCE, such as directors and, particularly, the company auditors, to pay them what they are legally due. (See also LITIGATION.)

DESCENT FROM HEAVEN
Amakaduri, literally a descent from heaven, refers to the practice, which was prevalent in some major Japanese companies, of appointing retiring bureaucrats from the regulatory bodies to well-paid sinecures, including directorships, when they retired. The same process can be seen in other countries, including France, where members of the *grandes écoles* fraternity move readily from government to corporate service.

DIFFERENT TYPES OF SHARES
Some companies create various classes of shares, under their ARTICLES OF ASSOCIATION, which have different terms such as preferential rights on a winding-up, priority to dividends, or special voting rights (see B SHARE). On the Shanghai and Shenzen stock exchanges in China "A shares" are available only to Chinese residents, whereas "B shares" are available only to foreigners. On the Hong Kong stock exchange "H shares" refer to shares of mainland Chinese companies listed there. (See also DUAL CLASS SHARE.)

DIRECTOR
A member of the board of directors, formally nominated and appointed by the members of the company at a properly convened meeting in accordance with the ARTICLES OF ASSOCIATION of that company. Some people may have a title including

the word director – marketing director, ASSOCIATE DIRECTOR, director of administration and so on – without necessarily being formal members of the board.

DIRECTORS' COMPETENCES

It is amazing that directors, the most important decision-makers in many organisations, often have little or no training for the job, neither are the core competences they need well understood. Apart from personality traits, such as integrity, intelligence and motivation, directors need to have basic competence in communication, decision-making, networking, political astuteness, strategic reasoning and strategic imagination. In addition, of course, all directors need to know enough about the organisation and the commercial, competitive context of the company's business to make a professional contribution. (See the MTRC case study in Appendix 3 and also CONFORMANCE ROLES and PERFORMANCE ROLES.)

As every business leader knows "our people are our most valuable asset". So why are they not on the balance sheet? (But) then there are those companies where a frank assessment would require the chairman to add: "our people are our biggest liability". Often the biggest liabilities sit on the board.

Editorial, *Accountancy*, September 1997

DIRECTORS' CONTRACTS

It is important to distinguish between contracts that executive directors might have as employees of the company and their contracts as directors. The Greenbury Report proposed that directors' contracts should run for no more than a year. Thus directors who had performed poorly and were replaced would not receive a gigantic GOLDEN HANDSHAKE on the termination of a long-term contract. Previously many British directors had rolling contracts of three years or longer. The requirement is now incorporated in the London

Stock Exchange's Code of Best Practice (see Appendix 4).

> *The pleasant but vacuous director need never worry about job security.*
>
> Warren Buffet, chairman of Berkshire Hathaway

DIRECTORS' REMUNERATION

This is a hot topic. Institutional investors in the United States have for some years been challenging directors' remuneration packages that are felt to be excessive when related to corporate performance. In the UK the issue has come to the fore as a result of investigative journalism and SHAREHOLDER anger.

In 1995 a group of City of London institutions commissioned Sir Richard Greenbury to look into board-level pay. The Greenbury Report proposed a Code of Conduct, the main recommendations of which were:

- companies should create a REMUNERATION COMMITTEE consisting solely of independent non-executive directors;
- the chairman of the remuneration committee should respond to shareholders' questions at the AGM;
- annual reports should include details of all director rewards, naming each director;
- directors' contracts should run for no more than a year to avoid excessive golden handshakes;
- share option schemes for directors should be linked to long-term corporate performance.

These recommendations have now been incorporated into the London Stock Exchange's Code of Best Practice (see Appendix 4).

One of the problems of determining directors' remuneration is the absence of relevant benchmarks, although *The Times* does now produce an annual report of directors of UK listed companies who are "over and under paid", using published data on salary, bonus, gains from options, annualised long-term incentive payments and other rewards. The key criteria for any remuneration committee should be corporate performance, measured in terms of growth in profitability, business potential and SHAREHOLDER VALUE in both the long and short term, against relevant norms that take into account the total reward structure of directors of similar companies in the same industry facing similar risks and career expectations. Such criteria should not be influenced by rewards offered to pop stars, footballers or entrepreneurs who have created their own businesses, or by remuneration levels in other countries, unless there is a real possibility of the directors in question being able and invited to work there. In other words, the remuneration benchmarks should avoid the effects of REMUNERATION RACHETING.

The 1995 AGM of British Gas, a privatised public utility, attracted one of the largest turnouts of shareholders in UK experience, one of whom brought along a pig called Cedric. The pig was named after the managing director whose 71% rise in remuneration package plus bonus, which coincided with voluntary redundancies and growing customer complaints, was the cause of concern. Nevertheless, the board, with the support of institutional investors, managed to secure the rejection of resolutions criticising its performance.

DIRECTORS' REPORT AND ACCOUNTS

Almost all company law jurisdictions now require the directors to submit regular reports and accounts to all shareholders (the exceptions are havens such as the British Virgin Islands). Their form and content has been progressively widened and sharpened through company law and by the regulatory requirements of bodies such as the US SECURITIES AND EXCHANGE COMMISSION, the Australian Securities Commission and the Hong Kong Securities and Futures Commission.

DISCLOSURE

Directors have a FIDUCIARY DUTY not to make a SECRET PROFIT out of their position in their companies. Consequently, they are required to disclose any interests they might have in matters being considered by the board. For example, if a director had a significant stake in a company in line for the award of a contract, the director must disclose that interest. The chairman and the board can then decide whether any action is necessary, such as asking the director not to comment or to leave the room when the issue is discussed. Directors declaring an interest should always ensure that it is minuted so that their hands are clean should there be a subsequent legal challenge.

DISQUALIFICATION OF DIRECTORS

Most company law jurisdictions provide for the disqualification of directors. Causes can include failure to meet the requirements of the companies legislation, running a company that has traded while insolvent, theft and fraud. In 1997 the Department of Trade and Industry in the UK disqualified 1,219 directors.

The board's real role is to support the leader – whoever he is, chairman or CEO. If my board was absolutely divided I would put the matter to a vote: but all those who vote against me should resign.

The opinion of a dominant director

DOMINANT DIRECTOR

Sometimes a company reflects the entrepreneurial drive of one person, often the founder. In such cases the board, while able to offer advice which might be heeded, is often overshadowed by the dominant director. Bill Gates of Microsoft and Richard Branson of Virgin Airlines are just a few examples of dominant corporate leaders. But although dominant directors may take their companies to the highest levels of achievement, unless they can cope with the succession problem they ultimately fail. The list of those who failed to provide for their succession is endless and includes Henry Ford, "Tiny" Rowland of Lonhro and Robert MAXWELL. Unfortunately, experience suggests that dominant directors have great difficulty in working with a potential successor – "nothing grows under an oak tree". (See also DUALITY.)

DREXEL, BURNHAM, LAMBERT

The Wall Street securities trading firm that in the 1980s was at the heart of the predator takeover market using junk bonds and was the base for the insider dealing activities of Ivan BOESKY, Dennis LEVINE and Michael MILKEN. In 1988 the firm pleaded guilty to six securities felonies and paid a record $650m in restitution. In 1990 Drexel filed for the protection of the Bankruptcy Court.

DUAL CLASS SHARE

Classes of shares with different voting rights are used to preserve the overall power of the incumbent family or other interests when the need for additional EQUITY capital threatens to dilute their opposition below that necessary for absolute control (see B SHARE). For example, following a hostile takeover attempt in 1953, the famous Savoy/Claridges Hotels group protected itself with a second tier of shares carrying 20 times the voting power of the ordinary, listed shares. The company was finally sold to American investors in an agreed sale in 1998. Dual class shares are prohibited in some jurisdictions and stock exchange listing committee rules.

DUALITY

One of the ongoing debates about the UNITARY BOARD is whether the role of chairman of the board should ever be combined with that of the chief executive officer (CEO). In Australia the roles in public companies are usually separated. In the United States many major companies combine the roles. In the UK the conventional wisdom, reasserted by the CADBURY REPORT, is that it is better to have the roles separated to avoid the possibility of a strong individual unduly dominating both managers and directors. The arguments in favour of splitting the roles are that two heads are better than one, but (more importantly) that duality provides a check and balance mechanism. Shareholders, particularly if there are minority interests, may find that a dominant leader, who is both chairman and CEO, has no one to keep him or her under control. The alternative view is that single-minded leadership can produce better performance. The results of research into the alternatives seem to be that under single leadership a company can do better, at least for a while, but that where the subtle relationship between the chairman and the CEO works well, major companies thrive better in the longer term.

An extension of the duality argument is whether a CEO should ever be appointed chairman of the board after retirement. It often happens. The proponents talk of retaining his experience; the newly appointed chief executives more typically fear that, although now chairman, their predecessor may not be able to let go of the managerial ropes.

The classic argument against the chairman being the former CEO is that the chairman will be a meddler. The CEO doesn't need that, of course, but he does need someone to confide in, to talk candidly about changes and other important matters. People in top positions need someone they can talk with openly and honestly.

Warren Bennis, in "Across the Board",
National Association of Company Directors Newsletter, 1993

DUTY OF CARE

Most legal systems impose on directors, either through statute, case law or regulation, a duty to exercise reasonable care, diligence and skill in their work. Directors are expected to bring to their director-level responsibilities the degree of care that could reasonably be expected, given their qualifications, know-how and experience. The interpretation of what constitutes reasonable care depends on the background of the individual. If directors are accountants, engineers or lawyers, then the degree of care expected of them would take their qualifications into account. But even if they have no such qualifications, the standard of professionalism now expected of directors around the world is significantly higher than it was a few years ago. Courts can act if fraudulent or negligent behaviour is alleged or where there are apparent abuses of power or suppression of the interests of minority shareholders. For example, courts will give a ruling if it is alleged that the directors have negotiated a contract that is detrimental to the interests of the minority. But, broadly, courts will not act to second-guess board-level business decisions taken under circumstances of normal commercial risk, should they subsequently prove to have been ill-judged.

EMPIRE BUILDING
(See GAMES DIRECTORS PLAY.)

EMPLOYEE DIRECTOR
Proponents of industrial democracy argue that governing a major company involves an informal partnership between labour and capital, and that consequently labour should be represented in the CORPORATE GOVERNANCE processes. A German SUPERVISORY BOARD, for example, has half of its members chosen under the co-determination laws through the employees' trade union processes. In the 1970s the draft fifth directive of the European Community (now the European Union) proposed supervisory boards with employee representation for all large companies. The BULLOCK REPORT was the British response. Since then the company law harmonisation process in the EU has been overtaken by social legislation, including requirements that all major firms should have a works council through which employees can participate in significant strategic developments and policy changes. Most members of the EU have adopted this legislation. The UK initially opted out, but the Labour government seems more sympathetic. Some major British firms with a presence in continental Europe have had to introduce works council procedures in their continental operations. They find there are repercussions as their British employees demand equal rights.

EMPLOYEE REPRESENTATION
See EMPLOYEE DIRECTOR.

EMPLOYEE RETIREMENT INCOME SECURITY ACT
In the United States the Employee Retirement Income Security Act (ERISA) of 1974 lays down fiduciary responsibility rules for all those who exercise control over the assets of employee retirement benefit plans. The Pension and Welfare Administration, which administers and enforces the act, has laid down criteria (in the frequently referred to "Avon letter") which require the fund managers to act in the best interests of the plan

beneficiaries, and not to use their proxy votes in companies in any way that is not in the beneficiaries' interests. This legislation also prevents directors calling on the proxy votes of shares held by their company's pension funds to promote or protect their own positions.

EMPLOYEE SHARE OWNERSHIP

Employee share ownership is sometimes advanced as a means of ensuring employee commitment. Instead of capital hiring labour, the argument runs, employees use capital. The governance processes of such companies typically involve employee nominated members. Employee share ownership plans (ESOPS) are most advanced in the United States, United Airlines being a good example. US tax laws allow ESOPS generous tax relief. In the UK the John Lewis Partnership is the most frequently cited example of employee ownership.

For over 80 years John Lewis (a leading UK retail chain) has been committed to the sharing of knowledge, power and gain among its employees, who are Partners in the business. Today, 34,000 Partners participate in the task of managing our business to serve customers better, and they share in the profits of our success. We believe this gives us commercial advantage and distinctiveness in a highly competitive sector.

Stuart Hampson, chairman, John Lewis Partnership, quoted in the *RSA Inquiry – Tomorrow's Company*, 1995

EQUITY

The share capital in a company that carries voting rights, and consequently the power to influence the CORPORATE GOVERNANCE of the firm. Most shares carry one vote and some stock exchanges prohibit non-voting shares and the DUAL CLASS SHARE (see also B SHARE); others do not.

ERISA

See EMPLOYEE RETIREMENT INCOME SECURITY ACT.

ESOP

Short for employee share ownership plan (see EMPLOYEE SHARE OWNERSHIP).

I have no problem with ethical issues, I merely ask myself whether I would mind if my old mother read about this in the press.

The company chairman of a British public company

ETHICAL FUNDS

Investment funds, such as mutual and unit trusts, run by INSTITUTIONAL INVESTORS dedicated to investing in companies that meet certain ethical criteria, such as providing environmental benefits or not trading in weapons, polluting processes or deforestation. Thus far such funds wield little power, other than raising awareness.

Failed leaders were being revealed in every walk of life… sad examples of excess, greed, and cynicism… I was profoundly disappointed at how frequently the graduates of some of our finest business and law schools were involved, in one way or another, in the cases being brought before the SEC. Surely we could do better.

John Shad, previously chairman of the SEC

ETHICS

As markets and business have become global and more open to international scrutiny, more attention has been paid to corporate ethics. Well-publicised financial scandals, such as those involving Ivan BOESKY, Dennis LEVINE, Michael MILKEN and Robert MAXWELL turned the spotlight on corporate social responsibility. Environmental tragedies, such as Union Carbide's plant explosion in Bhopal, which killed and maimed many people in India, and the Exxon Valdez oil spill in Alaska, sharpened the focus. Increasingly, public opinion demands that boards of directors exercise their considerable powers for good or harm with responsibility and in the interests of the many who can be affected, rather than solely in the interests of shareholders and the short-term bottom line. Understandably, some directors feel that their job is to ensure that the company is profitable and obeys the law and that if a society wants companies to behave in a specific way it must pass legislation to that effect. But ultimately a directorship is a position of trust, demanding absolute integrity, including the ability to make moral judgments, recognising the broader societal interests that can be affected by board decisions, and distinguishing the company's interests from personal interests.

One of the problems of a board dominated by executive directors is that they are marking their own examination papers.
Lord Caldecote, when chairman of the Delta Group. Had he been commenting today, he might have added: ...
and worse, many of them are awarding themselves the prizes.

EXECUTIVE DIRECTOR
A member of the board who is also employed by the company in a management capacity. As executives such directors are employees of the company, with rights and duties under employment law. As directors, however, they are responsible like all other directors under company law: the law makes no distinction between types of directors. One of the major challenges to an executive director is to be able to separate the two roles. On the one hand to perform as a member of top management running the enterprise; on the other to be a member of the board, jointly responsible with the other directors to see that it is being run well and in the right direction.

Executive directors have a special responsibility to inform the board on issues where the executive has special and relevant knowledge. In addition, executives as executives have primary responsibility for managing the corporation.
The Hilmer Report, *Strictly Boardroom*, Australia, 1993

EXECUTIVE SUPERVISION

Executive supervision involves the monitoring of management performance throughout the company and is one of the key elements of the board's activities. With a UNITARY BOARD, particularly if the executive directors are in the majority or dominate board proceedings, objective monitoring and evaluation of executive performance may be diluted. Strong chairmanship of the board is then needed. With the supervisory or TWO-TIER BOARD structure this responsibility falls to the upper, SUPERVISORY BOARD. In fact many unitary boards devote the greater part of their time and effort to this function, with their board papers mainly reporting financial results and recent operating data. Such a concentration on the CONFORMANCE and compliance role of the board, consequently, allows less time for the PERFORMANCE responsibilities of the board.

FAMILY DIRECTOR

A director of a company in which the controlling shares are held within a family. A family company is frequently a CLOSELY HELD COMPANY during the lifetime of the founder. On succession, however, differences can arise. Some shares may pass to members of the family who are no longer involved in management, although they remain non-executive directors. They want profits and dividends. They are concerned about expensive benefits available to the executive directors. Another conflict can arise if the second and third generations of the family expect to provide the senior management, whereas the company really needs to recruit professional management.

> *We may not do much good, but at least we don't do any harm.*
>
> Fin Guinness commenting on the role of the family directors in Guinness, quoted by his brother Jonathan Guinness, in *Requiem for a Family Business*, 1997

FIDUCIARY DUTY

Directors in all jurisdictions are expected to act with honesty, integrity and candour towards their companies, in particular towards the interests of the shareholders. This fiduciary duty is to the company as a whole, to both minority and majority shareholders, should they exist. In practice this can be difficult for a nominee director or when a dominant parent company exercises power over a subsidiary where there are minority outside shareholders. British Commonwealth-based common law (in Australia, Canada, India, New Zealand, Singapore, South Africa and so on) allows directors to determine the best interests of the whole company, subject to the right of appeal to the courts. Directors of companies incorporated in US states owe specific fiduciary duties to any minority shareholders. In other words, the primary duty of a director is to act honestly in good faith, giving all shareholders equal, sufficient and accurate information on all issues affecting their interests.

The underlying (and universal) principle is that directors should not treat a company as though it exists for their personal benefit.

FIGUREHEAD
One of the roles a director can play (see PERFORMANCE ROLES).

FUND MANAGEMENT
The management of investment funds such as mutual funds and unit trusts. Many now call for such INSTITUTIONAL INVESTORS to be involved in SHAREHOLDER ACTIVISM (see the 1998 HAMPEL REPORT, for example). They should exercise their voting rights, the argument goes, police recalcitrant boards, act as mediator on behalf of all shareholders when necessary and above all support the creation of shareholder value. But fund managers are not a homogeneous group. At one end of the scale are RELATIONSHIP INVESTORS and at the other are those mutual funds or unit trusts which have a purely short-term orientation; between these extremes lies the bulk of fund managers around the world.

The issues of power and accountability were raised at the outset in relation to corporate boards. They will increasingly be raised in the context of the growing power and relative lack of accountability of institutional investors. Their exercise of power over boards will only be seen as legitimate if it is open and reflects the views of those who have entrusted their money to them.
Sir Adrian Cadbury, *Directors' Monthly*, US, 1998

G

GAMES DIRECTORS PLAY

Although routinely presented as a serious, analytical and rational process, boardroom behaviour is often intensely political, involving interpersonal rivalries, corporate power-plays and networking skills. The games include the following:

- **Alliance building** is a power game played outside the board room for ensuring mutual support within. It is closely allied to log rolling.
- **Coalition building** involves canvassing support for an issue informally outside the boardroom so that there is sufficient consensus when the matter is discussed formally inside the boardroom.
- **Cronyism** is supporting a director's interests even though they may not be in the best interest of the company. For example, a director declares a personal interest in a contract in a tender being discussed by the board; he might even leave the room for the discussion. Board members support his bid, however, because of their relationship, even though it is not the most worthy.
- **Empire building** is the misuse of privileged access to information, people or other resources to acquire power over organisational territory. The process often involves intrigue, battles and conquests.
- **Log rolling** occurs when director A agrees, off the record, to support director B, on a board matter concerning B, for mutual support when it comes to a matter of interest to A.
- MEETING MANIPULATION
- **Snowing** involves executive directors deluging an OUTSIDE DIRECTOR seeking further INFORMATION with masses of data, thus confusing the situation and papering over any cracks.
- **Rival camps** is a game played when there are opposing factions on a board, in which hostilities, spies and double agents can be involved.

- **Sponsorship** is support by one powerful director for another, usually for their joint benefit.
- **Suboptimisation** occurs when a director argues for the benefit of part of the organisation to the detriment of the company as a whole. Some directors, particularly executive directors, suffer from tunnel vision because they are too closely involved with what is going on and from myopia because they will be personally affected by the outcome. An independent evaluation of top management performance by outside directors can help to overcome such problems.

Strong chairmanship can reduce the opportunities for game playing.

Power concedes nothing without a demand. It never did and it never will.
Johnnie L. Cochran Jr, *Journey to Justice*, 1996

"In my experience ..." is one of the most over-used phrases in board-level discussions. The question that should always be asked is whether that experience is relevant to the subject in hand.

As they say in board meetings "trust me on this".
Peanuts

GENERIC STRATEGY
A description of the overall strategic stance of a business. For example, a company might adopt an overall generic strategy that differentiates its products or services from the competition, perhaps by product characteristics, quality, or service; or the overall generic strategy may be to focus on a specific niche in the market, a boutique operation, perhaps; or the company could rely on its scale, cost-efficiency and market positioning to compete on price with a low-cost strategy. Further, in terms of strategic options, a company may look to

expand through internally generated growth and may be focused on local, regional or international markets. Or it could be genuinely global, locating procurement, manufacturing, assembly, sales and marketing, servicing and financing wherever it is commercially and strategically viable.

GERMAN CORPORATE GOVERNANCE

Public companies in Germany have a TWO-TIER BOARD governance structure: an upper, SUPERVISORY BOARD (the *AUFSICHTSRAT*) and the executive board or committee (the *VORSTAND*). The supervisory board requires the executive board to present its proposals and plans to it for comment and approval, then reviews and assesses subsequent managerial performance. The Netherlands has also adopted the two-tier structure and it is permissible in France.

Under co-determination practices in Germany, major organisations are believed to require a close relationship between capital and labour. Consequently, supervisory boards have equal numbers of representatives of the shareholders and of the employees. Common membership of supervisory and executive boards is not permitted. The power of the supervisory board lies in its ability to appoint and remove executives from the executive committee. In the Netherlands the supervisory board has a tripartite structure: capital, labour and public interest.

Another feature of governance in major German companies is the role of German banks as major shareholders.

GOLDEN HANDSHAKE

A bountiful reward given to directors on the termination of their contracts, often negotiated when the contract was first signed. Such rewards are sometimes criticised because the extent of the handshake bears no relation to the contribution the director has made to the company; sometimes the reverse. (See also DIRECTORS' CONTRACTS and DIRECTORS' REMUNERATION.)

GOLDEN HELLO

A one-off payment made to a director as an incentive to join a company, typically recognising some of the benefits forgone by leaving the previous company and acknowledging the additional costs and risk involved in the move.

GOLDEN PARACHUTE

A device written into some executive directors' contracts which enables them to float away from the company with exorbitant severance pay, should specific circumstances, such as a successful takeover, arise.

GOLDEN SHARE

A share in a company that gives overall power over the company to its owner, but only if a specific situation, such as a takeover bid, occurs. The most usual cases are in corporatised or privatised companies operating in fields such as power, transport or telecommunications. When privatising a public-sector business, the government may retain the right (perhaps for a set number of years) to activate its golden share to stop control passing to a foreign corporation.

GOVERNING BODY

Every CORPORATE ENTITY needs to be governed and the governing body fulfils that need. In the case of a JOINT STOCK LIMITED LIABILITY COMPANY the governing body is typically the board of directors. In other corporate entities it may be called the council, the senate, the executive committee, even the governing body. Most of the ideas and insights in this book can be applied to such bodies.

GOVERNING DIRECTOR

A phrase used mainly in Australia to describe a director with dominant powers in a PRIVATE COMPANY. Although the legislation requires such companies to have two directors, the statutes do not prevent companies from framing their ARTICLES OF ASSOCIATION to give virtually all powers to one person: the governing director.

GREENMAIL

Arbitrageurs who buy shares on the possibility of a takeover bid, with the intention of bidding up the price to sell at a profit, or acquiring a sufficient stake to block the bidder and force one side or the other to buy the shares at a premium to obtain control, are indulging in greenmail.

GREENBURY REPORT

See DIRECTORS' REMUNERATION.

HAMPEL REPORT

This 1998 report from the Committee on Corporate Governance, chaired by Sir Ronnie Hampel, is a successor to the British CADBURY and GREENBURY reports. Its preliminary report in 1997 listed a set of principles of CORPORATE GOVERNANCE, which reflected current conventional wisdom on corporate governance principles for listed companies. In the final report three prevailing themes emerged:

- that good corporate governance needs broad principles not prescriptive rules. Compliance with sound governance practices, such as the separation of board chairmanship from chief executive, should be flexible and relevant to each company's individual circumstances and not reduced to what the report calls a "box-ticking" exercise. Self-regulation is the preferred approach: no more company legislation is needed.
- that the board is accountable to the company's shareholders. There is no case for redefining directors' responsibilities to other stakeholder groups.
- that the UNITARY BOARD is totally accepted in the UK. There is no interest in alternative governance structures or processes such as two-tier boards.

Predictably, perhaps, a committee composed predominantly of directors of major public companies and their professional advisers did not criticise contemporary corporate governance, nor did it advocate any measures which would further limit directors' power to make unfettered decisions, nor widen the scope of their accountability. Shortly after the report was published the British government announced a new fundamental review of UK company law.

HARMONISATION OF COMPANY LAW

There have been attempts in a number of jurisdictions to encourage the convergence of company law. Australia and Canada have developed business laws at the federal level, provoking adverse reactions from the states and provinces involved which feared a loss of autonomy and tax revenue. The European Union has also had a company law harmonisation programme for many years, although this has been largely overtaken by social legislation affecting CORPORATE GOVERNANCE issues in recent years (see also EMPLOYEE DIRECTOR). In the United States companies can be incorporated only in individual states; there is no federal companies' legislation, only securities legislation. This is one reason why companies incorporate in states such as Delaware, which have reasonably liberal company laws.

> *In corporate governance, we shall work for less regulation and against the idea of a permanent standing committee, which would most likely look for ways of interfering with and regulating corporate activity.*
> Tim Melville-Ross, secretary general,
> Institute of Directors, London, 1997

HELICOPTER VISION

An essential requirement of every director: the ability to perceive issues at different levels of abstraction. When a helicopter is on the ground the pilot can see every blade of grass but cannot see very far. As the helicopter rises so more and more comes into the pilot's vision, but in less and less detail. At a considerable height it is possible to see to the distant horizon and scan all the ground in between, but the detail of individual elements has now been lost.

So it is with directors' thinking. Helicopter vision involves being able to think, for example, at the level of the personalities involved in a situation, at the level of a department, STRATEGIC BUSINESS UNIT or subsidiary, or the company as a whole, or the industry, internationally or even globally. Some people, perhaps because of their professional training or earlier experience, think only at a single level. They do not make good directors. Those who can perceive issues at different levels are of board potential.

But the greatest challenge to a director is not just to have helicopter vision; many people can achieve this with experience. The difficult part is to decide which level is appropriate to the matter at hand. Far too many decisions are made at an inappropriate level. Perhaps a decision is treated as an operational matter, failing to recognise the managerial or strategic aspects; or the reverse, the decision is treated as strategic, failing to recognise the operational implications.

HILMER REPORT

A report of a committee of The Sydney Institute, published as *Strictly Boardroom* in 1993. (The title reflects the film "Strictly Ballroom" in which competitive ballroom dancing had become so regulated that innovation was stifled.) This, says the report, is what can happen to CORPORATE GOVERNANCE. It advocated an emphasis on the PERFORMANCE ROLES of the board.

> *The board's key role is to ensure that corporate management is continuously and effectively striving for above-average performance, taking account of risk. This is not to deny the board's additional role with respect to shareholder protection.*
> The Hilmer Report, *Strictly Boardroom*, Australia, 1993

IASC
See INTERNATIONAL ACCOUNTING STANDARDS COMMITTEE.

ICGN
See INTERNATIONAL CORPORATE GOVERNANCE NETWORK.

INDEMNITY INSURANCE
The need for personal indemnity against the threat of LITIGATION is becoming important in many parts of the world. Litigation brought by shareholders and others alleging misfeasance, breach of duty, negligence or other actions in damages, against companies, their boards, their auditors and, particularly, against individual named directors has been increasing. The predilection towards litigation began in the United States but has spread; auditors and directors in Australia, the UK and other countries are now increasingly subject to lawsuits that may involve huge claims for damages. Nowadays it is sensible for directors to ensure that they are adequately covered by indemnity insurance. Sometimes referred to as D&O (directors and officers) insurance, such cover offers some protection against legal costs and damages awarded. In some jurisdictions directors have to pay their own premiums since, it is argued, a company may not use its own funds to protect its directors from their own negligence.

INDEPENDENT DIRECTOR
An OUTSIDE DIRECTOR or NON-EXECUTIVE DIRECTOR with no interests in the company, other than the directorship, which might affect, or be seen to affect, the exercise of independent judgment. Some regulators, such as the SECURITIES AND EXCHANGE COMMISSION in the United States, lay down detailed criteria to determine independence. Essentially, however, a director cannot be seen to be independent if he or she (or a company with which they are connected) has had significant business dealings with the company (for example, as a supplier, agent, customer, or banker), or if he or she is closely related to the chairman or a member of top management, or

was previously an executive of the company. Although there may be a good case for people with such connections or experience to be on the board, they cannot be considered to be fully independent, and hence cannot be part of the check and balance mechanisms enshrined in the AUDIT COMMITTEE, the NOMINATION COMMITTEE or the REMUNERATION COMMITTEE.

INDUCTION PROGRAMME

An induction programme can provide a new director with valuable INFORMATION and training. Although often "promoted" to the board for their successful executive performance, many executive directors have little knowledge and experience of board-level work. Conversely, a NON-EXECUTIVE DIRECTOR is likely to have little knowledge of the company and its industry. The purpose of a director induction programme is to speed up the time at which a director can really contribute to the board. (See the induction checklist for new directors in Appendix 1.)

I find that it takes a director up to a year before he really understands what is going on in board meetings, and another year before he really contributes anything worthwhile.
Chairman of a major UK company

INDUSTRY ANALYSIS

STRATEGY FORMULATION has to be competitor- and customer-based and is often global in context. For many directors industry analysis is the starting point for thinking about corporate strategy. Michael Porter, a professor at Harvard Business School, has outlined five driving forces of competitive analysis (see Figure 11).

Taking an industry perspective rather than a narrower, more self-centred one, has changed the strategic battlefield for many boards. No longer are they constrained by thinking primarily about their own products and services and how to market them. Now they focus primarily on the needs

The driving forces of competitive advantage

- Threat of new entrants
- Power of suppliers
- Existing rivals in the industry
- Power of buyers
- Potential substitute products and services

Source: Michael Porter, 1980.

11

of customers and potential customers. They review the strategies being pursued by their competitors. They identify potential new competitors and think about what barriers there are to entry into the field. They consider what developments, perhaps in technology, delivery systems or new products, might cause customers to change their allegiance. In other words, many directors are now thinking strategically, before they get down to approving plans for their own companies.

One of the difficulties of industry analysis is determining the boundaries of the industry. Industries overlap: telecommunications and computers; information technology hardware and software; retail banking and financial services. STRATEGIC ALLIANCES increasingly cross traditional industry frontiers. Potential competitors may come from what appeared to be a non-competing industry.

INFORMATION

Directors have the right to the information they feel is necessary for them to fulfil their responsibilities as directors. Some chairmen make a great effort to ensure the directors of the company are provided with the information they need, through both formal board papers, board and individual briefings and an INDUCTION PROGRAMME. But in some companies directors are provided with no more than standard packs of data for board meetings, with inadequate information, much of which is tabled during the meeting. There are now some computer-based information systems available that enable directors to gain access to relevant director-level information. (See also WAR ROOM.) Improving the quality of board information and an increasing use of information technology will be crucial in improving BOARD EFFECTIVENESS in the future.

INSIDE INFORMATION

Confidential information about a company's affairs known only to those with access to the company. Using such information to buy shares to make a profit or sell shares to prevent a loss is INSIDER DEALING.

> *Private information is practically the source for every large modern fortune.*
> Oscar Wilde, *The Ideal Husband*

INSIDER DEALING

Trading in a listed company's shares on the basis of privileged, share-price sensitive INSIDE INFORMATION is a breach of a director's FIDUCIARY DUTY. It is also illegal in most countries, although it has only recently been made so in Japan, Hong Kong and Germany. But successful prosecutions for insider dealing are few because it is often difficult to prove that a particular transaction was made as a result of inside information. The United States has the most severe penalties for insider dealing.

The argument against the practice, whether buying shares in the secret knowledge of events that would drive the price up, or selling shares to avoid a loss given secret intelligence on events that would cause the price to fall, is not so much that it is unfair, or because it involves a misuse of information, but because insider dealing destroys the credibility and the integrity of the market.

Directors of listed companies have to be particularly careful not to trade in their company's shares when they are in possession of inside information, such as the company results just prior to publication and before the stockmarket has that information. The COMPANY SECRETARY should inform directors when the window of opportunity for trading in the company's shares is open and, more importantly, when it is closed.

I think public comment can be a very dangerous way of working for an institutional shareholder. We are here to enhance the value of people's money. We wouldn't in any way want to cause problems by making comments in public.

Lawrence Burr, managing director, NSW State Superannuation Investment and Management Corporation, Australia, *Company Director*, 1993

The most important question raised by the emergence of the pension funds, and other institutional investors, as the main suppliers of capital and the majority owners of the large business is their role and function in the economy. Their emergence makes obsolete all traditional ways of managing and controlling large business. It forces us to think through and redefine the governance of companies.

Peter Drucker, *Post-capitalist Society*, 1993

INSTITUTIONAL INVESTOR

A financial institution with shareholdings in listed companies. Institutional investors include pension funds, investment trusts, mutual funds (or unit trusts), life and other insurance companies and banks running investment portfolios for clients. The proportion of institutional investor interests in EQUITY shares has been increasing throughout the world, and in some major markets is now well over 50%. Often institutional investors show little interest in the CORPORATE GOVERNANCE of the companies in which they invest, preferring to take a short-term perspective and "vote with their feet" if they are dissatisfied with a company's performance. Some FUND MANAGERS, however, have taken a stand in specific cases and voted their shares accordingly. In the early 1990s this resulted in major board changes at American Express, General Motors and IBM. Some institutions have been prominent in such developments, including CALPERS (the Californian State Employees pension fund) and the UK-based Pension Investment Research Consultants (PIRC). (See also RELATIONSHIP INVESTOR.)

INTERLOCKING DIRECTORSHIP

Sometimes called a cross-directorship, this is where directors sit on each others' boards. In certain circumstances, such as in a STRATEGIC ALLIANCE, there can be benefits in cross-directorships. But generally the practice is suspect because of the often undisclosed concentration of power. Many studies, particularly in the United States, have analysed the structure of cross-directorships. These can involve complex networks of linkages as well as direct A on B's board and B on A's board links. (See also *KEIRETSU*.)

INTERNATIONAL ACCOUNTING STANDARDS COMMITTEE

Founded in 1973 "to formulate and publish in the public interest accounting standards to be observed in the presentation of financial statements and to promote their international acceptance and observance". The International Accounting Standards Committee (IASC), with 128 member bodies from 91 countries, is working in liaison with IOSCO to produce a set of international accounting standards which will facilitate cross-border listing of companies. However, compliance with the IASC by companies in the United States and the UK, which promulgate their own standards, is low. Further convergence can be expected.

INTERNATIONAL CORPORATE GOVERNANCE NETWORK

An organisation of major investment institutions

from 15 countries, representing $130m of investment, created in 1995. Among the activities of the International Corporate Governance Network (ICGN) are the identification of international best practices in corporate governance and recommendations on ways to eliminate barriers to cross-border share voting.

Attacking the barriers to cross-border voting is a powerful new demand from US institutions to vote shares worldwide.

Stephen Davis, *Global Proxy Watch*, 1997

INTERNATIONAL ORGANISATION OF SECURITIES COMMISSIONS

The International Organisation of Securities Commissions (IOSCO) is a voluntary organisation of financial regulators from over 50 countries, whose members regulate more than 98% of securities traded worldwide. Regular meetings have lead to many agreements to co-operate, including the exchange of information. Thus the regulation of financial markets and the monitoring of abnormal trading in shares have global dimensions. It is increasingly difficult to bury INSIDER DEALING through transactions in overseas markets.

IOSCO

See International Organisation of Securities Commissions above.

JAPANESE CORPORATE GOVERNANCE

In the companies within Japanese *KEIRETSU* the board plays a formal, even ritualistic role. Boards are large and almost entirely executive. Komatsu, for example, had 26 board members: the chairman, the PRESIDENT and executive vice-president, three executive managing directors, three managing directors, 14 other directors and three statutory board auditors. Canon had 26 and Toyota 55 board members. In effect the board is the top four or five layers of the management organisation. Promotion to the board, as in the West, is a mark of distinction; but, unlike the West, interpersonal competition, which has been a feature of life throughout the organisation, continues on the board for promotion to the next level. Senior managers seem often to be younger than their Western counterparts.

The commercial code calls for "representative directors" to be elected by the board. Whereas, from a Western viewpoint, these might be expected to represent the interests of various stakeholders in the firm, their actual role is to represent the company in its dealings with outside parties such as the government, banks and other companies in the industry. Typically, the representative directors include the chairman and president and other top directors.

The code also calls for the appointment of individuals as full-time statutory auditors. They report to the board on any financial problems or infringements of the company code or the company articles. They can call for information from other directors and company employees and can convene special meetings of the board. These internal board-level auditors, of course, liaise with the external professional auditors.

Non-executive directors in the Western sense would be unusual. A few of the executives might have served with other companies in the *keiretsu* added-value network, and in that sense may be able to represent the interests of suppliers or downstream customers; others might have been appointed to the company's ranks on retirement from the *keiretsu*'s bankers or even from among the industry's government regulators (known as a DESCENT FROM HEAVEN). There are no independent, outside directors, no audit committees of outside directors, no remuneration committees and certainly no two-tier boards with employee representation as in Germany.

The Japanese do not see the need for intervention "from the outside". Indeed, they have difficulty in understanding how outside directors function. People who have spent their lives in a company wonder how outsiders could possibly know enough about it to make a contribution. How could they be sufficiently sensitive to the corporate culture, which has been created over the executive directors' business lifetimes? Worse, might they not damage the harmony of the group by failing to appreciate its subtleties?

Considering board styles, the social cohesion within the Japanese firm is well known. The high levels of unity throughout the organisation have been widely noted, together with non-adversarial relationships, lifetime employment, enterprise unions, personnel policies which emphasise commitment, initiation into the corporate family, cross-functional training and promotion based on loyalty and social compatibility as well as performance, even though some of these attributes are now threatened following recessionary pressures in Japan. Equally well known is the approach to decision-making by consensus, involving a lengthy process of discussion and negotiation throughout the organisation before agreement is reached.

The board consequently tends to be a decision-ratifying body rather than a decision-initiating and decision-taking forum, as in the West. Meetings of the entire board are often ceremonial, with honourable titles used on social occasions, although this aspect of society is in transition. Meetings of the managing directors with the directors in their teams are crucial. More significant, in governance practice, seem to be the informal relationships among the top echelons of the board.

*The path to the Japanese board has changed little
over the past 40 years. There is only one route
and it begins on the first day a new employee,
fresh from university, arrives at the corporate
offices… Elevation to the rank of director (is) the
supreme reward for competent service, but with
little modification in managerial
responsibilities… Eventually many departmental
heads are again promoted becoming
simultaneously head of an operating unit and a
"managing director". Even the "senior managing
directors" are heads of divisions or important
staff departments. These are masquerade boards
in which managers briefly don
the masks of directors.*

Aron Viner, "The Coming Revolution in Japan's Board Rooms",
Corporate Governance, Vol. 1, No. 3, July 1993

JOINT STOCK LIMITED LIABILITY COMPANY

A CORPORATE ENTITY formally incorporated under
the company law of a given jurisdiction, with a
legal existence separate from its owners, whose
liability for the company's debts is limited to their
EQUITY stake. It is a very simple and clever idea
from the mid-19th century which underpins
CORPORATE GOVERNANCE. Without companies there
would be no need for directors.

*Just whose liability is limited in the limited
liability company?*

A member of the Royal Family on taking up a non-executive
directorship.

The answer is the shareholders, not the directors.

JOINT VENTURE

See STRATEGIC ALLIANCE.

JUDGE

One of the roles a director can play (see CONFORM-
ANCE ROLES.)

KEIRETSU

Networks of Japanese companies connected through inter-trading, cross-directorships and cross-holdings. Often the network includes a financial institution. Chairmen and senior directors of companies in the *keiretsu* meet regularly and have close, informal relationships. (See also CROSS-HOLDING and INTERLOCKING DIRECTORSHIP.)

KING REPORT

A South African committee, under the chairmanship of Mervyn E. King, published a code of corporate practices and conduct in 1994, based on a broad consensus of the South African corporate community. The report includes a "code of ethics for enterprises and all who deal with enterprises".

LEAD DIRECTOR

An approach adopted by General Motors (see Appendix 5) and some other major companies, in which an outside director is chosen to chair meetings of the outside directors. Another use of the term can be found in companies with complex business interests, where individual directors are given a portfolio of interests on which they take the lead in board meetings. For example, one director might lead on new product development, marketing in a specific product group and management of one of the group's international regions.

LEGAL DUTY

Directors have two fundamental duties under the company law of almost all jurisdictions: a FIDU-CIARY DUTY to act with honesty, integrity and candour towards the members of the company; and a duty to exercise reasonable care, diligence and skill in their handling of company matters.

LEVINE, DENNIS

Dennis Levine, when in his 20s, found that INSIDER DEALING was easy and apparently foolproof. As a bank employee he had access to information about prospective financial deals. Exchange that knowledge with an executive in another bank who knew about that bank's deals; open an account in a Swiss bank and trade under a false name in the Bahamas and, bingo, the compliance authorities would never know. Later, although earning over $2m legitimately from his employment with the US finance house DREXEL, BURNHAM, LAMBERT, he grew over-confident – some might say greedy. He took a position in American National Resources Company on the basis of a potential bid which his own company was preparing. He made $1.3m, but he underestimated the capabilities of government investigators and the co-operation of securities regulators (see IOSCO). Mr Levine agreed to give evidence against his colleagues, pleaded guilty and was sentenced to two years imprisonment and a fine of $362,000 on felony charges. In addition he had to make restitution to the SECURITIES AND EXCHANGE COMMISSION of $11.6m in alleged insider trading profits. Further, he had to agree to an injunction barring his employment in the securities business for life. (See also BOESKY and MILKEN).

LIMITED LIABILITY
See COMPANY LIMITED BY GUARANTEE, CORPORATE ENTITY, JOINT STOCK LIMITED LIABILITY COMPANY.

LISTING RULES
The regulations that each stock exchange lays down governing the minimum requirements for having a company's shares listed on that market. Typical listing rules include requirements on the contents of prospectuses, on reports and accounts to members, and on matters of board membership, over and above the requirements of the company law in the jurisdiction of incorporation. For example, the New York Stock Exchange requires listed companies to have an AUDIT COMMITTEE; London requires the annual report to state whether the requirements of the code of best practice in CORPORATE GOVERNANCE have been fulfilled; and Hong Kong insists on two independent non-executive directors. The ultimate sanction for failing to meet the listing rules would be a refusal to list or a delisting. But since this would disenfranchise minority shareholders and penalise the market, which the listing rules are predominantly intended to protect, such sanctions are usually threats used in discussions rather than actions carried out in practice.

LITIGATION
A growing part of corporate life. Audit firms, companies, boards and individual directors are increasingly being exposed to claims for damages in actions brought by shareholders, bankers, customers and others, alleging losses arising through negligence, usually when a company has run into financial difficulties. Courts will seldom second-guess the business judgment of boards; however,

that does not prevent aggrieved parties bringing actions. In the United States, which has become the most litigious nation in the world, the threat of legal actions is affecting the preparedness of people to serve as outside directors. Even if the INDEMNITY INSURANCE cover is adequate, directors can still face the aggravation of a legal action and the personal embarrassment of media exposure. Some companies, and particularly their auditors, having faced massive claims for damages because of the DEEP-POCKET SYNDROME, can find indemnity insurance prohibitively expensive or even unavailable.

LOG ROLLING
See GAMES DIRECTORS PLAY.

LONG-RANGE PLANNING
See BUDGETARY PLANNING.

M

MAXWELL AFFAIR

Robert Maxwell (born Jan Ludvik Hoch in Slovakia in 1923) grew up in poverty, fought with the Free Czech army and received the British Military Cross. He became an international publishing baron. In the early 1970s British government inspectors had led an inquiry into the Maxwell company Pergamon Press and concluded that he was not "a person who can be relied on to exercise stewardship of a publicly-quoted company". Nevertheless, he succeeded in building a media empire founded on two public companies: Maxwell Communication Corporation and Mirror Group Newspapers. When he died at sea in mysterious circumstances on November 8th 1991, it was alleged that he had used his dominant position as chairman of the trustees of the group's pension funds to siphon off funds to support his other interests, and that he had been involved in an illegal scheme to bolster the price of companies in the group. Eventually, the lead companies were declared insolvent and the group collapsed. Independent accountants, called in to investigate for bank creditors, estimated that £763m had been plundered from the two public companies and their pension funds and used to prop up Mr Maxwell's private interests.

There are many lessons for directors in the Maxwell affair. Mr Maxwell's leadership style was dominant: he reserved considerable power to himself and kept his top executives in the dark. An impressive set of non-executive directors added respectability to the PUBLIC COMPANY boards, but were also ill informed. He threatened LITIGATION to prevent public discussion and criticism of his corporate affairs; many investigative journalists and one doctoral student received writs. The complexity of the group's organisational network, which included both listed entities and private Maxwell companies, many incorporated in tax havens like Liechtenstein and Gibraltar with limited disclosure requirements, made it difficult to follow transactions and to obtain a comprehensive overview of group affairs. The group's auditors,

Coopers and Lybrand, were criticised by the accountancy profession's Joint Disciplinary Scheme and were sued for alleged negligence. The role of the trustees of the group pension funds was brought into question. The powers and processes of the regulatory bodies, including the Department of Trade and Industry, the SERIOUS FRAUD OFFICE, the Investment Management Regulatory Authority, the Stock Exchange and the OCCUPATIONAL PENSIONS BOARD, were also shown to be insufficient in practice to police Mr Maxwell's dealings.

MEETING

Directors carry out many of their functions in meetings of the board and its subcommittees. Consequently, effective meetings are crucial to board performance. Yet many chairmen fail to realise that meetings need to be planned as well as run. The AGENDA is, typically, the chairman's prerogative. (See also CHAIR, MEETING MANIPULATION, MINUTES.)

MEETING MANIPULATION

Many board meetings call as much for political acumen and interpersonal skill as for analytical ability and rational argument. There are a number of devices which the skilful meeting manipulator uses to advantage.

- The management of the AGENDA provides a crucial opportunity: who controls the items to be discussed (and those to be avoided) controls the focus of the meeting.
- At the start of the meeting, challenging the MINUTES of the last meeting can be a device to reopen discussion of an item that was resolved against your interests last time. Then, should discussion of an item in the current meeting be running the wrong way, there are a number of devices to stall or refocus the debate.
- Talking around the subject to shift the discussion on to favourable issues is a

particular skill of meeting manipulators. Profound irrelevance is their stock in trade. But filibustering to run the discussion out of time will seldom work at board level.

- The put-down involves the skilful introduction of doubt when responding to a proposal before the board, as in: "We discussed this matter before you joined the board and decided against…" or "The bank would never agree with anything like that…" These are simple examples; good put-downs can be far more sophisticated.

- Presenting ideas in the context of other people's can be powerful: "I was inclined to believe… until I heard X, now I wonder whether we should…" The fact that X was advocating something quite different is irrelevant.

- Summarising the discussion so far can be used to emphasise favourable points and downplay others: "What the meeting seems to be saying is…"

- An extension of the summarising device is to predetermine the decision, preferably in Latin, as in: "We seem to have reached the decision, chairman, NEM. CON." Nem. con. (nemine contradicente, or no one against) can be suggested, whether anyone is actually against or not.

- Where a discussion is running in quite the wrong direction: "On a POINT OF ORDER, chairman…" is a call which, if offered with sufficient challenge and conviction, will stop an orator in full flight. Strictly, points of order only have relevance if there are standing orders about the running of meetings, but that should not deter skilful meeting manipulators. Argue that the discussion has strayed from the point of the agenda item, that extraneous issues are being raised, or that this discussion would be more appropriate under another item – anything to deflect the ongoing discussion.

- Calling for a postponement of the discussion

until the next meeting, on the grounds of lack of information, the need for more reflection, or until an absent member is present, can also be used to postpone a decision that seems to be running against your interests.

- Calling for an adjournment of the meeting is a heavier version of the postponement device.
- If the ARTICLES OF ASSOCIATION or the rule book of the corporate entity specify a QUORUM, keep your eyes on the number of people present. Lack of a quorum can always be used to stymie further debate.
- Finally, the management of the minutes provides a crucial opportunity to manipulate a meeting.

The meeting manipulator's advice to a new director would be to forget rationality and what you learned in your MBA programme: influence, not analysis, is what counts in directors' meetings. Ignore the apparent short-term issues, set out to discover the cliques and cabals, find out who wields what power over whom. Make your presence felt, but carefully: "I wonder whether we might consider ..." not "these financials are a load of rubbish". "In my experience ..." is a better start to a contribution than "Surely everyone knows that…" Propose alternatives rather than attack proposals on the table: "Another alternative might be…" rather than: "That'll never work in a month of Sundays." (See also GAMES DIRECTORS PLAY.)

MEMORANDUM OF ASSOCIATION
The formal, legal constitution governing a company. Typically, the memorandum will state the company's name, the location of its registered office, its objectives, that the liability of its members is limited and the structure of the EQUITY capital. Since a JOINT STOCK LIMITED LIABILITY COMPANY has a legal existence separate from its members, it is important for there to be a formal document that enables anyone contracting with the company to

know its precise legal status. Most company law jurisdictions require the memorandum, duly agreed by the founding members of the company, to be filed at the time of incorporation. Subsequent changes require the approval of the members.

MENTOR

An experienced member of a board who accepts a responsibility, usually quite informally, to induct and guide a new member into the ways of that board. The relationship can enable the new director to contribute more quickly and effectively.

MILKEN, MICHAEL

One of the key players in the predator takeover market in the United States during the 1980s, using high-return, high-risk junk bonds. Working for DREXEL, BURNHAM, LAMBERT, he was at the centre of the INSIDER DEALING ring that included Ivan BOESKY and Dennis LEVINE. Mr Milken and his brother were eventually indicted on 98 charges of racketeering and securities fraud. This was the world's biggest insider dealing case to date. He was fined the sum of $1 billion and served two years in jail. He was also banned from the securities industry for life (and subsequently fined a further $47m for breaking this probation order). He is now involved in a software training venture on the Internet.

MINUTES

The formal record of a MEETING. The COMPANY SECRETARY often keeps the minutes. Although there are no specific rules governing the content or format of minutes of board (or board subcommittee) meetings, they should provide a competent and complete record of what transpired and what was decided. Should there be any future challenge the minutes, duly approved as a true and fair report at a subsequent meeting, can be used as strong evidence of what was intended. Companies generally develop their own minute-keeping style; for example, some boards note the names of the key contributors to the discussion, others do not. In some cases the minutes are no more than a brief record of who attended and what was decided. At the other extreme, there are minutes that are almost a verbatim report of the proceedings, complete with stage directions. The ideal lies between the two. They should contain sufficient information to capture the key threads of the discussion, the alternatives considered, the agreement reached and plans for action. The person responsible for writing the minutes potentially wields considerable power. (See MEETING MANIPULATION.)

MISSION STATEMENT
A statement, usually approved at board level, of the underlying purposes of the company. A mission statement will, typically, include references to the various stakeholders in the business process; for example, suppliers, customers, shareholders, employees and, sometimes, broader societal interests. A well-developed mission statement can help the directors in the PERFORMANCE ROLES of STRATEGY FORMULATION and POLICY-MAKING, because it establishes the desired relationship between the company and other parties that might be affected by board decisions. The danger of mission statements is that they can become little more than a public relations exercise, exhorting the company to do well by all of its stakeholders without realising that their interests may be in conflict and without establishing the company's actual mission. (See also CORE VALUES.)

MONITORING MANAGEMENT
Monitoring and supervising executive management is one of the key components of a board's work. Indeed, many boards devote the major part of their time to this activity, perhaps to the detriment of the PERFORMANCE ROLES of STRATEGY FORMULATION and POLICY-MAKING. Another problem in monitoring management activity is striking the right balance between ensuring that management is pursuing the policies and plans agreed by the board, and avoiding domination of executive decision making.

Monitoring of management activities is often

financially oriented, using data generated by the internal management accounting systems and executive information systems. But increasingly boards are seeing that they need non-financial measures of performance on matters such as customer satisfaction, product development and employee morale. Financial measures can over-emphasise the short-term performance to the detriment of the board's responsibility for the longer-term development of the business. It is also important not to rely solely on routine and standard performance reports. Briefings and presentations from non-board executives can be valuable sources of orientation and information for directors, particularly outside directors. One of the challenges executive directors face in monitoring management is that, effectively, they may be monitoring their own performance. Possible solutions are effective non-executive directors, tough-minded chairmanship and a professional BOARD STYLE. (See also EXECUTIVE SUPERVISION.)

NAPF

See NATIONAL ASSOCIATION OF PENSION FUNDS below.

NATIONAL ASSOCIATION OF PENSION FUNDS

An organisation representing the interests of INSTITUTIONAL INVESTORS among British pension funds. The National Association of Pension Funds (NAPF) has taken a higher profile in CORPORATE GOVERNANCE issues in recent years, monitoring company activities against codes of good corporate governance conduct, occasionally advising on SHAREHOLDER ACTIVISM and PROXY VOTING options. (See also ASSOCIATION OF BRITISH INSURERS.)

Communication is key. In the past companies have not understood shareholders. They in turn have wondered why a company hasn't explained its actions adequately in its annual report.
David Gould of NAPF, proposing greater institutional investor involvement in corporate governance affairs

---

NEM. CON.

Short for *nemine contradicente*, which means no one speaking against or unanimously (see MEETING MANIPULATION).

NOMINATING COMMITTEE

A subcommittee of the main board made up wholly, or mainly, of independent outside directors, to make recommendations on new appointments to the board. It is an attempt to prevent the board being seen as a cosy club, in which the incumbent members appoint like-minded people to join their ranks. A check and balance mechanism designed to reduce the possibility of a DOMINANT DIRECTOR, such as the chairman or CEO, pushing through their own candidates. Nominating committees are widely used in major American companies. But it is interesting to note that the independent outside directors who form the committee are themselves often drawn from the ranks of CEOs and chairmen of other companies, and are therefore likely to recommend those of like mind.

On the other hand, as some observe, if the board is to work as a tough-minded, effective team, it is just as well that its members can get on together. In the UK, although most of the proposals of the CADBURY REPORT were quickly followed by the listed companies, the requirement to have a nominating committee has met with the greatest resistance. This is not surprising since the right to appoint to the board goes to the very heart of corporate power.

> *I am not happy with co-options to the board by the incumbent directors to fill casual vacancies that are put to the AGM merely for confirmation.*
> John Charkham of PRONED, the official UK organisation for the Promotion of Non-Executive Directors)

NOMINEE DIRECTOR
See REPRESENTATIVE DIRECTOR.

NON-EXECUTIVE DIRECTOR
A member of the board who is not employed by the company as an executive. The term is widely used in the UK and other countries in the Commonwealth such as Australia, Hong Kong and Singapore. In the United States the term more frequently used is OUTSIDE DIRECTOR. A basic tenet of good CORPORATE GOVERNANCE is that the non-executive directors provide checks and balances on the executive directors. To achieve that, however, the non-executive directors also need to be independent of the company. In other words they should have no relationship with the company that could be seen to influence the exercise of objective, independent judgment. This means that a director acting as a nominee for a major shareholder or a bank, or someone linked to a firm in the company's added-value chain such as a supplier or a distributor, a member of the chief executive's family, or a past employee of the company cannot be seen to be independent. There may be a good case for such people to serve on the board as non-executive directors, but they cannot be seen to be independent. Particular challenges for

non-executive directors are finding enough time to devote to the affairs of the company and knowing enough about the company's business and board-level issues.

> *Sir, You report that a prototype supermarket trolley has been designed with a self-centring steering system to eliminate "erratic trolley control". Perhaps it will also dispel my long-standing belief that the difference between a supermarket trolley and a non-executive director is that, while both hold a vast quantity of food and drink, only the trolley has a mind of its own.*
> *Yours, T. P. Blenkin, York*
> Letter to the editor, *The Times*, London, May 1997

> *Pet rocks*
> Ross Perot, when referring to the non-executive directors of a large American company

> *What we want are non-executive directors who are geese not frogs. Frogs will sit motionless in water that is heated to boiling point, unaware of their situation, and taking no action until their ultimate demise. Geese, as in Rome, honk loudly at impending crisis.*
> Christopher (Kit) McMahon, when deputy governor of the Bank of England

> *The division of responsibility between directors, auditor and senior management, is not sufficiently clear. The focus is almost entirely on defining the responsibilities of directors. Yet the commercial reality of the matter is that, in these days of conglomerates and perhaps trans-national conglomerates at that, the opportunity for non-executive directors to exercise meaningful control over management is as slight as the ability of ministers to control a vast bureaucracy...*
> Justice Andrew Rogers in the AWA case, Australia, 1992

NON-PROFIT DIRECTOR

A director of a non-profit enterprise (or, as some prefer, not-for-profit organisation, recognising that enterprises for profit do not always make a profit). These enterprises may be incorporated formally as companies limited by guarantee, in which case most of the material in this book will be relevant to their directors. Others may be created as trusts, in which case many of the insights and ideas can also be applied. A particular challenge to boards of non-profit entities is determining what performance measures are appropriate, given that the bottom-line profit criterion, by definition, does not apply.

NON-VOTING SHARE

A share which carries rights to contribute to and participate in the company's financial affairs but not the right to vote in company meetings. Such shares are not common and are usually offered to outside investors in companies in which control is held by one SHAREHOLDER (or a group of shareholders) who wants to retain a dominant position. Non-voting shares are not allowed under the LISTING RULES of most stock exchanges.

OCCUPATIONAL PENSIONS BOARD

An independent statutory body set up in the UK to ensure that pension schemes comply with statutory requirements and that pension schemes contracted out of the national procedures meet the minimum benefit requirements. It was caught out badly by the MAXWELL AFFAIR.

OUTSIDE DIRECTOR

A term used in North America to describe a member of the board who is not an executive employee of the company. The usage in the UK and most Commonwealth jurisdictions is NON-EXECUTIVE DIRECTOR. The term outside director implies a genuine outsider, that is someone who is independent of the company, with no relationships (other than the directorship) that might be seen to affect the exercise of objective, independent judgment.

But what about the board? These guys were the illustrious guardians of the Ford Motor Company. They were supposed to constitute checks and balances to prevent flagrant abuse of power by top management. But it seems to me their attitude was: "As long as we're taken care of, we'll follow the leader… There's one mystery I want to unravel before I die: How can those board members sleep at night?"

Lee Iacocca in his autobiography

The control of a large corporation is such a complex job and requires such constant attention that the outside board member, who has his own affairs to look after, can know very little about the business – too little on the whole to be useful as an outsider… And an outside director in a large corporation cannot know enough to be specific, he must remain a figurehead.

Peter Drucker, *Concept of the Corporation*

OWNERSHIP

Ownership is the basis of power in the Anglo-

American concept of the corporation. Formally, the shareholder members of the company nominate and appoint the directors, who have a duty to exercise stewardship over the corporation for the benefit of the shareholders and to be accountable to them. Reality can be rather different. In large public companies the membership is likely to be diverse, with both individual and institutional shareholders, whose objectives for dividend policy and capital growth differ, and who are scattered geographically. The ability of owners to exercise power in such circumstances is severely limited. Suggested alternatives include a TWO-TIER BOARD with the SUPERVISORY BOARD reflecting, among other things, shareholder interests, or a CORPORATE SENATE providing an intermediary shareholder committee. Increasingly INSTITUTIONAL INVESTORS are being expected to exercise their power on behalf of all the owners. STAKEHOLDER THEORY calls for a rethink of the essentially 19th century concept of the corporation to reflect 21st century societal needs.

In less than a century there is a serious question as to whether the modern corporate form has become obsolete ... How can one justify a system in which investors purchase shares in a company that is far too big and complex to permit any meaningful shareholder involvement in governance?

Robert A.G. Monks and Nell Minow,
Power and Accountability, 1991

PERFORMANCE ROLES

The second set of roles that every UNITARY BOARD and governing body must fulfil (see also CONFORMANCE ROLES). The performance roles involve STRATEGY FORMULATION and POLICY-MAKING.

The main performance roles of directors are as follows.

Wise man This involves bringing accumulated knowledge and experience to bear on issues facing the board. The director is drawing on past experiences in business and elsewhere. In other words the board is respecting the wisdom of the director. Long-serving directors may well find themselves cast in this role by newer board colleagues. Accumulated "wisdom" can of course have limitations in fast-changing situations.

Specialist The director relies on his or her particular professional training, skills and knowledge to make a contribution. For example, the specialism could be in the realm of accountancy, banking, engineering, finance or law; or it could stem from specialist knowledge of a particular market, technology or functional area such as marketing, manufacturing or personnel. In some newer, growing companies outside directors are appointed to the board specifically to provide specialist inputs until such time as the company can afford to acquire these skills in-house at the executive level. When a board is relying on such expertise, it is important to ensure that the director remains in touch with the subject; this can sometimes prove difficult for those operating at board level.

Window-on-the-world The director is being used as a source of information on issues relevant to the board discussions. Usually this will be on matters external to the company, such as insights into market opportunities, new technologies, industry developments, financial and economic concerns or international matters. Obviously it is essential that the information is relevant, accurate and current. This is often a role specifically sought from outside directors, who are in a position to obtain such information through their day-to-day activities. A danger is that directors, the choice of whom was influenced by their access to certain information, become out of touch without admitting to their colleagues that they are no longer as close as before.

Figurehead The director is called on to represent the company in the external arena; for example, in meetings with fund managers and financial analysts, or in trade and industry gatherings. The chairman of the board often takes on this responsibility, being invited to join public committees, commissions and the governing bodies of important public institutions, as well as joining the boards of other, non-competing companies. A figurehead is also increasingly important for many companies in dealing with the media.

Contact person This is an important role often played by outside directors, who are able through personal contacts to connect the board and top management into networks of potentially useful people and organisations. For example, the director might be placed to forge contacts in the world of politics and government; link the company with relevant banking, finance or stock exchange connections; or make introductions within industry or international trade. This role typically supplements the window-on-the-world role, but adds a more proactive dimension. Politicians are sometimes given directorships on the assumption that they have useful contacts and influence in the corridors of power.

Status provider In the past eminent public figures were often invited to join boards just to add status rather than because of any specific contribution they could make to board deliberations. A knighthood or elevation to the House of Lords, in the UK, or service as a senator in the United States, almost guaranteed invitations to join public company boards. In today's business climate, business acumen, professionalism and the ability to contribute directly to board affairs is vital. Moreover, exposure to LITIGATION deters some public figures from accepting merely honorary directorships. But even today, if a company has been experiencing some high-profile problems, it can help restore confidence if a status provider with a reputation for integrity is appointed to the board.

PEST ANALYSIS

A review of the Political, Economic, Social and Technological setting used in STRATEGY FORMULATION and POLICY-MAKING. Boards need information on the current and potential PEST context as they consider strategic options for their company around the world.

PETERS REPORT

A committee set up under the auspices of the VEUO (Association of Securities-Issuing Companies) and the VVDE (the Amsterdam Stock Exchange Association) reported in 1997 on corporate governance in Holland, a country which uses TWO-TIER BOARDS or SUPERVISORY BOARDS. The report made some forty recommendations on the composition, task, appointment, remuneration and method of working of both supervisory and executive boards. Better accountability, increased transparency and a more professional way of working were recommended for the Dutch supervisory system.

PIRC

Short for Pensions Investment Research Consultants. The PIRC has been a frequent source of SHAREHOLDER ACTIVISM in the UK, advising its clients of issues (such as allegedly excessive DIRECTORS' CONTRACTS or DIRECTORS' REMUNERATION) and recommending PROXY VOTING actions.

POINT OF ORDER

Some organisations establish formal rules for meetings which specify procedures for the orderly conduct of business. Typically, such rules provide for participants in the meeting to appeal to the CHAIRMAN on a "point of order" should they feel the rules are not being followed. (See also MEETING MANIPULATION.)

POISON PILL

A device for foiling a hostile takeover. For example, the terms of a company's ARTICLES OF ASSOCIATION may include provisions that:

- reduce the voting power of any shares once a holder acquires, say, 30%;
- provide a high-return security to existing shareholders should a bid not be recommended by the board;
- introduce convertible stock on which the conversion terms change on an unwelcome bid.

POLICY-MAKING

Policies enable strategies to be implemented. For example, a company may need a set of market policies that lay down the ground rules on matters such as pricing, service and customer relations. Without such policies, management might well take decisions that were contrary to the STRATEGIC INTENT. Product policies might be needed to cover issues such as product safety, innovation and quality. Financial policies might cover credit and debt collection, borrowing limits and gearing, spending controls and management approval limits, inventory control and working capital management. Employment policies might lay down the criteria for worker safety, pay and conditions, and the company's attitude towards trade unions. Some companies have written policies for social responsibility, which detail the firm's commitment, for example, towards minority rights, pollution control or the environment generally.

Policy-making is one of the key elements of the board's PERFORMANCE ROLES. In business circles it is usual to talk of policies stemming from strategies. For example, a company, having decided to pursue a strategy of product differentiation, will need appropriate pricing policies, customer relations policies and product safety policies. In government circles the terms tend to be reversed; for example, a government talks of pursuing a policy of tax reduction through various strategies such as cutting tax rates or through higher allowances.

PORTFOLIO ANALYSIS

A professional CORPORATE PLANNING technique which enables directors to locate their product portfolio in a matrix comparing market share (and thus the ability to generate cash flow) with market potential (the likelihood of growth). A jargon has grown up around portfolio methods. Firms were enabled, for example, to identify and distinguish their products as "stars", "cash cows", "dogs" and those with "potential". Star products had high market share and continuing potential; cash cow products also had large market shares but their life cycle was in decline, so they could be milked to provide the funds to invest in those products which had potential, but as yet low market share. Dogs had neither current market standing nor future potential and should be removed from the portfolio. Such methods were based on a belief that all products had life cycles, which should be reflected in corporate strategies. Experience has shown that although portfolio analysis can give directors some useful insights, it does not produce strategies. The theory of product life cycles was found to be over-simple and, organisationally, it proved difficult to find managers who were prepared to see the profits which they had created "milked" to feed other parts of the company.

PRESIDENT

A title often held in conjunction with the chairman. The precise responsibilities and powers vary considerably. It is more widely used in American companies than elsewhere.

PRESIDENT DIRECTEUR-GENERAL

The powerful sole head of many French companies in which the UNITARY BOARD is normal but not mandatory.

PRIVATE COMPANY

Many company law jurisdictions differentiate between a PUBLIC COMPANY and a private company.

Private companies, typically, are not allowed to make public invitations to subscribe for shares and have to limit the number of shareholders (50 in the UK). In recognition of their special status, the regulatory requirements for private companies, for example on the filing and disclosure of information, may not be as demanding. Some jurisdictions have a further subcategory of private company for the small or CLOSELY HELD COMPANY, in which the owners, directors and managers are closely related. Further relaxation of the regulatory requirements may apply, for example, over the need for AUDIT.

PRIVATISATION

Since the mid-1980s there has been a trend around the world towards corporatising and privatising enterprises that had previously been run as nationalised industries. Examples include telecommunications, power utilities, water supply, airlines, railways and shipping. The corporatisation step involves the creation of a CORPORATE ENTITY with a board of directors to run the business on market-oriented, profit-driven criteria. Typically, at this stage, the government still makes the appointments to the board and sets the investment and performance criteria. The privatisation stage involves selling all or part of the EQUITY on the stockmarket. Now the shareholders, who of course may still include the state, have a say in the appointment of the directors and the assessment of their performance. All the issues of CORPORATE GOVERNANCE and BOARD EFFECTIVENESS apply to privatised companies. There may, however, be an additional set of challenges brought about by the monopolistic position of, say, privatised utilities and also when there is a requirement for a privatised company to provide universal service; for example, to supply remote areas at below true market cost. Such challenges are usually tackled through the establishment of a REGULATOR, but also through government subsidies.

Privatisation is used in a completely different context to describe the actions of the directors and majority shareholders of a public listed company when they decide to make the company private by buying back those shares that are in the hands of the public.

PRODUCT MAPPING

A tool of CORPORATE PLANNING which enables directors to locate their portfolio of products, product groups or strategic business units in the context of their competitors, using whatever criteria they think appropriate, for example, by availability, distribution channels, quality, market recognition, service characteristics, or price.

PRONED

An organisation for the promotion of non-executive directors, initiated by the Bank of England and other City of London institutions to encourage the wider use of independent non-executive directors in public and other companies in the UK. PRONED undertook an exhortatory role and provided a NON-EXECUTIVE DIRECTOR appointments service. Subsequently, a similar organisation was formed in Australia.

PROXY VOTING

In a PUBLIC COMPANY shareholders typically have the right to appoint proxies to vote on the resolutions before general meetings of shareholders. In earlier times this typically meant voting on the reappointment of directors and auditors, accepting the annual accounts and agreeing the dividend to be paid. In recent years, particularly in the United States and increasingly in the UK, dissatisfied shareholders have used the proxy mechanism to promote their concerns, calling for the removal of chairmen and chief executives, attacking the level of DIRECTORS' REMUNERATION and introducing other critical resolutions.

PUBLIC COMPANY

A company that is permitted to invite public subscription for its shares. By definition all companies listed on a stock exchange are public companies; but a public company need not be listed, attracting its shareholders (such as venture capitalists) by other means. Recognising the benefits a public company enjoys, most jurisdictions require more extensive filing, disclosure and IN-FORMATION access than is required of a PRIVATE COMPANY. In the early days of the corporate concept, in the 19th century, all companies were public companies. Today, although public companies are often the more significant firms and some of them are huge, they account for less than 5% of all companies in number.

QUASI-GOVERNMENT ENTERPRISE
The move towards cost-effectiveness in government in many countries has led to developments such as corporatisation, PRIVATISATION and outsourcing. One result has been the creation of various quasi-governmental institutions to facilitate, monitor and regulate these activities. Many of the issues of CORPORATE GOVERNANCE discussed in this book apply to the members of such boards, committees and councils, even though they may not have the formal title of director.

QUORUM
The minimum number of members who need to be present, under the ARTICLES OF ASSOCIATION or other rules of the CORPORATE ENTITY, to legitimise the meeting or "make it quorate". (See MEETING MANIPULATION.)

REGULATOR

A state-wide or federal company registrar function is necessary in all company law jurisdictions to ensure that companies are properly incorporated, listed on the company register and continue to meet such requirements as filing periodic returns and financial reports. The office of the company registrar provides one of the basic controls in CORPORATE GOVERNANCE. For a PUBLIC COMPANY listed on a stock exchange, the listing committee of the exchange also exercises a control function ensuring compliance with that exchange's LISTING RULES. Regulators are often also appointed to oversee specific industries that have been privatised.

RELATED PARTY TRANSACTION

A business transaction between a company and parties closely related to it, such as directors or major shareholders; for example, the purchase by a company from one of its directors of a building or shares in another company. The LISTING RULES of most stock exchanges require related party transactions to be disclosed and, often, approved by the other shareholders.

RELATIONSHIP INVESTOR

An INSTITUTIONAL INVESTOR who takes a significant, long-term stake in a listed company with a view to being closely involved and intending to have a close relationship with the board. Examples include Warren Buffet, whose Hathaway fund invests in no more than a handful of companies for the long-term and intends to exercise some influence over the company, and Robert Monks, whose Lens Fund also takes a long-term position with a view to developing a close relationship with the company. Sometimes the relationship investor will have a REPRESENTATIVE DIRECTOR on the board. While some might argue that relationship investing represents a return to the original concept of shareholder democracy, it has to be noted that when a single investor has a close relationship with the company and is able to influence the board, the other shareholders will not have that inside information or influence.

> *A good director is one who has a meaningful
> financial stake in the venture … (as) there is
> nothing that makes a director think like a
> shareholder more than being a shareholder.*
> Warren Buffet, Berkshire Hathaway

> *Relationship investing contrasts sharply with the
> stereotype of the American shareholder who is
> depicted as an off-track bettor with no interest in
> the horse beyond the results for the daily race.
> "Betting slip" shareholding is not a promising
> base for responsible ownership. The combined
> status of ownership and commercial relationship
> gives particular investors a sufficiently significant
> stake to ensure an effective presence.*
> Robert A.G. Monks, "Relationship Investing",
> *Corporate Governance*, Vol. 2, No. 2, April 1994

> *I've always said my favourite time frame for
> holding a stock is forever. I don't buy stocks with
> the idea of selling them unless I'm in arbitrage…
> I only invest in companies within my circle of
> competence: I don't mind missing opportunities
> from firms I don't understand.*
> Warren Buffet, speaking at Harvard Business School

REMUNERATION COMMITTEE

A committee of the main board, consisting wholly
or mainly of independent, outside or non-executive directors, responsible for overseeing the
remuneration packages of the other directors and,
possibly, members of senior management. DIREC-
TORS' REMUNERATION has been an issue of concern
around the world. In the United States it has been
a particular focus of institutional and relationship
investors, who have commended the notion of
remuneration committees but noted the potential
problem where even independent non-executive
committee members are themselves executive
directors of other companies and therefore have a
vested interest in high benchmarks. In the UK, the

Greenbury Report was specifically directed to the issue and recommended the wider use of remuneration committees. Elsewhere, including Australia and Hong Kong, there has been much debate about the extent of director rewards and the manner in which they are paid (salary, fee, bonus, options, benefits in kind and so on).

REMUNERATION RACHETING

Directors use various arguments to justify high board-level rewards. These include:

International comparator   "To ensure that our company attracts and holds executive directors of the calibre we need against international competition, we have to pay salaries that are broadly comparable to those they could obtain in the industry anywhere in the world." This argument is advanced even if the directors concerned have never been headhunted in their lives and whether or not they have any possibility of working abroad.

Headhunter   "We have just recruited a new executive director and the headhunters assured us that he had to receive a package that is 30% more than that of the highest-paid director. Of course, we all had to have an increase to maintain differentials." This argument conveniently overlooks the fact that the fee of the headhunter is based on 30–35% of the first year's salary of the new appointee.

Top of the industry   "Our firm prides itself on being one of the leaders in the industry, even though at the moment we are not among the most profitable. We expect to pay our directors in the upper quartile of the industry range as shown by the comparator pay research." This argument totally ignores the performance of the firm or the directors.

Fear of loss   "We stand to lose our directors to the competition unless we pay competitive rates." This argument is sometimes advanced even though the directors concerned are within a year or two of retirement and would be of absolutely no interest to competitors.

Doubling up the bonus "We believe that it is important for directors' rewards to be perform-ance related. Moreover, we expect excellent performance in both the short and the long term. So we calculate bonuses on the annual profits, then we have a parallel three-year scheme which rewards directors if earnings per share (or profit against budget) grow by 30% over that period." This way the directors get rewarded twice on the same performance, inflation is ignored and there is no upside cap should there be exceptional cir-cumstances. Moreover, directors do not get penalised for poor performance.

In the UK, the United States and some other countries there are now specialist consultants who offer advice to companies on appropriate levels of reward. Some also advise the fund managers of INSTITUTIONAL INVESTORS who are, increasingly, monitoring DIRECTORS' REMUNERATION and taking action when it seems out of line. (See also REMU-NERATION COMMITTEE.)

Directors' remuneration lies at the heart of the corporate governance debate in the eyes of 90% of the British population ... Most outside directors are not remuneration experts and are conscious of the need to maintain harmony with their executive colleagues ... If governance protocols cannot be seen to tackle this problem adequately it will fail to prevent the imposition of statutory controls over the next 20 years.
Peter M. Brown, chairman of the Top Pay Research Group, 1993

REPRESENTATIVE BOARD
A board whose members are the direct nominees of specific members or appointed to represent the interests of various groups of members. An exam-ple would be the committee of an agricultural co-operative in Canada whose members represent growers, buyers and sources of finance.

REPRESENTATIVE BOARD STYLE

A form of BOARD STYLE in which directors act on behalf of the interests of specific shareholders or stakeholders. Representative boards are frequently found in non-profit entities, where the directors are elected to serve the interests of various interest groups (for example, in a hospital trust, on behalf of the patients, the doctors, the nursing staff, the Health Authority, even the local community).

RESPONSIBILITIES OF DIRECTORS

See FIDUCIARY DUTY and DUTY OF CARE.

REPRESENTATIVE DIRECTOR

A director who is acting as a nominee for a major SHAREHOLDER or other stakeholder, such as a venture capitalist or bank with funds invested in the company. The position of such a nominee can be fraught with difficulty because all directors have a primary duty to act for the good of the entire body of shareholders and not to take the part of any particular interested party. Furthermore, directors have a duty not to disclose privileged information that is not available to the body of shareholders as a whole. In practice it is important for directors who have been nominated and appointed to represent specific interests that their position is understood by the other directors and, should a seriously contentious situation arise, that they take legal advice.

In Japanese company boards the concept of the representative director is the reverse; there the director is so called because he represents the company in its dealings with the government, competitors and other companies in the *KEIRETSU* network. (See JAPANESE CORPORATE GOVERNANCE.)

RIVAL CAMPS

See GAMES DIRECTORS PLAY.

ROLES FOR DIRECTORS

Although all directors have the identical responsibility to act for the good of the company, in practice different members of the board will play different roles according to their knowledge, experience and expertise. In fact directors should be appointed for the different qualities they can bring to the job, whether they are technical skills or excellent contacts. (See CONFORMANCE ROLES and PERFORMANCE ROLES.)

> *I no longer want to sit on large boards where the non-executive directors have largely symbolic roles. I want to learn and make a real contribution. If I take on a non-executive directorship, I will always do my best to attend board meetings, to read the papers and to take a real interest in the company concerned.*
> Sir Dennis Henderson

RUBBER STAMP BOARDS

A form of BOARD STYLE in which directors act solely to confirm decisions taken by executive management or the holding company in a group.

SAFETY VALVE
One of the roles a director can play (see CONFORM-
ANCE ROLES).

SBU
See STRATEGIC BUSINESS UNIT.

SCENARIO BUILDING
Another tool of CORPORATE PLANNING which is used
by some firms to look ahead, to identify social,
economic, political or technological developments that would have significant implications for
the strategic future of the firm, and to develop pictures of possible outcomes. Various techniques
have been developed to produce such scenarios,
including teams of experts, "futurology" and sim-
ulation modelling. Such methods are still in use in
some industries, including oil and gas exploration,
refining and distribution, although scenario building failed to predict the oil crisis of the 1970s, the
collapse of the Soviet Union and the rapid and
dramatic effects of the personal computer.

SEC
See SECURITIES AND EXCHANGE COMMISSION.

SECRET PROFIT
A director must not make a secret profit out of
dealings with the company, for example through
private interests in a contract in which the company is involved. Directors have a duty to disclose
such interests to the board and to abide by its decision as to what is in the company's best interest.

SECURITIES AND EXCHANGE COMMISSION
A US body, set up under the Securities Exchange
Act of 1934, to protect shareholders from over-
ambitious company promoters and unscrupu-
lously powerful incumbent boards. Over the years
the disclosure, regulatory and investigative powers of the Securities and Exchange Commission
(SEC) have increased and the United States now
has the most expensive (and the most litigious)
corporate regulatory regime in the world.

SERIOUS FRAUD OFFICE

The Serious Fraud Office (SFO) is the British government body that investigates and prosecutes serious or complex corporate fraud. Its success rate has not been high.

SHADOW DIRECTOR

Occasionally a company has a dominant individual, often the founder and significant shareholder, who wields power over company affairs although he is not actually on the board. For example, when new legislation was introduced in Hong Kong, requiring the disclosure of directors' shareholdings and remuneration, a number of prominent individuals resigned from their boards, thus avoiding the revelation of personal information. It was apparent, however, that they continued to exercise considerable power over the remaining directors. Such people are called shadow directors. Although they are not formally directors, the other board members operate in their shadow. In some jurisdictions shadow directors can be held responsible for certain actions in the same way as a formally appointed director.

SHAREHOLDER

The owner of shares in a company. There may be various classes of share, such as ordinary EQUITY shares (giving single or dual class voting rights), preference shares (giving preferential rights to dividend and/or on winding up) and other types of investment instrument. The vital thing for the director is to be aware of the voting rights and terms of each class, as described in the ARTICLES OF ASSOCIATION, because that determines the ultimate governance power in the company, even though crucial voting may seldom occur. (See also B SHARE and DUAL CLASS SHARE.)

SHAREHOLDER ACTIVISM

In a private, CLOSELY HELD COMPANY the shareholders and the directors are often close, even the same people, and consequently the shareholders can readily influence board decisions.

Around the commercially advanced world, however, individual shareholders in public companies seldom have real power in governance matters. In the major listed companies, shareholdings are widely dispersed and geographically spread. Even with SHAREHOLDER interest groups and better opportunities to communicate with the other members, individual investors lack the position, prestige or power to influence an incumbent chairman and the board. RELATIONSHIP INVESTORS seek to overcome this problem.

But an INSTITUTIONAL INVESTOR, even with a small holding, can influence the board, particularly if it acts in concert with others. However, the interests of different types of institutional investor do not necessarily coincide; for example, some may be looking for a quick profit, while others may take a longer-term view. There is also the potential problem, if institutional investors get too close to directors, that share price-sensitive INSIDE INFORMATION may be passed.

> *Electronic reporting will become the norm for companies, enfranchising the ultimate owners of capital, leading to cheaper costs of capital and ultimately driving a democratisation of shareholder relations.*
>
> Paul Myners, chairman,
> Gartmore Investment Management plc

SHAREHOLDER VALUE

The boards of many listed companies are committed to maximising the value of their shareholders' EQUITY, a commitment reinforced by the HAMPEL REPORT. But the measurement and management of shareholder value is not a straightforward accounting calculation. There are a number of methodologies used, including value-based management (VBM), economic value added (EVA) and shareholder value added (SVA). But, essentially, all measurements of shareholder added-value recognise that historical, profit-based measures fail to take into account the cost of the capital that has been used and offer variations on measures of the present value of future cash flows, discounted at the average cost of capital. Trends in share prices and dividend pay-out are often taken as a short-term surrogate for shareholder value.

As ever, the problem in shareholder value analysis lies in making the concept work in practice. While there are as many theories as business school professors, implementation often proves elusive.

Nigel Masters, in *Accountancy*, May 1998

SHELL COMPANY
A company listed on a stock exchange whose shares are not currently being regularly traded. On some stock exchanges, if control is acquired over such companies, the listing can be used to obtain a quotation for other business enterprises without incurring the expense and exposure of a full prospectus by "backing" the other business into the shell company. This is sometimes called a "backdoor listing".

SNOWING
See GAMES DIRECTORS PLAY.

SOKAIYA
A member of a *YAKUSA* gangster organisation in Japan, used to disrupt annual general meetings of companies. *Sokiya* were originally employed to ensure that no awkward questions were asked by individuals (the average length of shareholder meetings in Japan is still just over 15 minutes). But sometimes disputes arise over their remuneration and trouble ensues. A famous meeting of the Sony Corporation lasted 13 hours with chairs as well as abuse being thrown.

SPECIALIST
One of the roles a director can play (see PERFORM-ANCE ROLES.)

SPONSORSHIP
See GAMES DIRECTORS PLAY.

The old cry of 'what about the workers?' is being replaced by a new call 'what about the stakeholders?' But it is important to distinguish directors' accountability from their responsibility.

Andrew Pettigrew, Warwick Business School, November 1997

STAKEHOLDER THEORY
A body of ideas pursued in the 1970s and early 1980s. In the Corporate Report, a study commissioned by the UK's accounting bodies in 1975, it was suggested that major corporations had a duty to be accountable to all those who might be affected by their actions, including employees, suppliers, customers and communities, as well as shareholders. The political dimensions of the proposals resulted in considerable criticism and the shelving of the proposals. Ira Millstein and Salem Katsch, writing in 1981, offered the following insight into the issues:

> *This strident and partisan concept of substantially unrestrained corporate power and discretion is, in a more moderate form, among the most important fundamental public concerns within large corporations ... at issue is whether the nation ... will accept larger private corporate size, accelerate the decline of pluralism by regulating or by giving greater responsibility to government, or by requiring fundamental changes in the internal governance structure of our major corporations.*

Stakeholder thinking faded in the free-market, growth attitudes of the 1980s, but it is now re-appearing. (See TOMORROW'S COMPANY.)

STATUS PROVIDER
One of the roles a director can play (see PERFORMANCE ROLES).

STEWARDSHIP THEORY

The original theory underpinning company law: directors can be trusted to pursue their FIDUCIARY DUTY to the company, acting as stewards of the shareholders' interests, which they place ahead of personal ambition. In this stewardship theory runs contrary to the ideas of AGENCY THEORY which holds that individual directors, given the chance, will maximise their own utility and cannot be expected to adopt a stewardship perspective if checks and balances are not put in place.

> *No business exists in a vacuum. We are conscious of the influence our business has on communities throughout the UK, both locally and nationally. If a community as a whole flourishes, the individual members of that community tend to flourish too.*
>
> Sir Colin Southgate, chairman, Thorn EMI, quoted in *RSA Inquiry – Tomorrow's Company*, 1995

STOCK OPTION

The right to acquire the shares of a company some time in the future at a pre-determined price. Much used, in the remuneration package of executive directors and, increasingly, outside directors, as a motivator and reward for improved performance. Hermes, one of the UK's largest fund managers, has suggested that non-executive directors should receive half their post-tax remuneration in shares.

STRATEGIC ALLIANCE

Strategic alliances with other companies are the preferred way for many companies to enter markets, transfer technology, procure supplies or manufacture products around the world, or share risk on an international scale. Sometimes the partners in the strategic alliance are competitors in other fields. Many alliances involve the incorporation of a joint-venture company owned by two or more partner companies. Directors of such joint-venture companies are typically drawn from the senior management of the partners. Governing joint-venture companies can present special challenges. Disagreements not envisaged in the initial joint-venture agreement can arise between the partners. Directors then face conflicts of interest between their responsibilities to the joint-venture company and to the partner company which employs them. Moreover, many joint-venture companies are incorporated in foreign jurisdictions, with diverse and different company laws and regulatory regimes, and have overseas partners with different cultures.

STRATEGIC BUSINESS UNIT

A favourite organisational approach of major western companies is to create separate organisational divisions that are strategically responsible for profit performance in specific product and market areas. The rationale is that the management of these strategic business units (SBUs), by concentrating on the performance of given strategic sectors, will maximise the benefits to the group as a whole. Doubt has been thrown on the validity of this approach by observing the practices of some Japanese companies which make the CORE COMPETENCES of the group available across the entire product portfolio.

Of the eleven companies named as Britain's most profitable by Management Today between 1979 and 1989, four subsequently collapsed and two were acquired.
RSA Inquiry – Tomorrow's Company, 1995

STRATEGIC INTENT

The underlying drive of a board of directors to achieve strategic success in the longer term. It might be, for example, to become the largest company in the software industry, to be the best airline in the world or to put a specific competitor out of business. Strategic intent enables a company to make the most of its CORE COMPETENCES, to establish CORE VALUES throughout the organisation that unite everyone to the common goal, and to achieve better results than would have occurred had the board merely sought to fit the company's resources to the strategic situation.

STRATEGIC VISION

Directors need a shared perception of the future for their company; a perspective that encapsulates their aspirations for the enterprise. Some call this a strategic vision. It reflects what the board wants to achieve; the direction it wants the organisation to take; where it wants the enterprise to be in the future. "When you don't know where you're going, all roads lead you there."

Information about the strategic context is obviously fundamental to this process. One of the important developments in the provision of INFORMATION at board level in recent years has been the creation of customer and competitor information systems, monitoring not what is going in inside the company, as most traditional management information systems do, but what is going on outside in the strategic milieu. Sometimes a strategic vision is articulated in no more than a general statement of overall aims; in other cases quantified aims or goals are determined.

But a strategic vision remains no more than a dream unless management can turn it into reality. Strategies have to be formulated that suggest ways in which the strategic vision might be achieved in practice.

STRATEGY FORMULATION

Setting the direction for the business, in the context of the external competitive and customer market situation, and in the light of prevailing economic, political and technological factors. This is a crucial aspect of the board's role; it is after all why directors are so called.

Strategy formulation is typically an iterative process leading from perceptions of the strategic situation, through possible strategies, choices, projects, plans, implementation and outcomes. Strategic thinking is ongoing. Strategies tend to emerge over time rather than be created by a deliberate planning process.

During the 1970s and 1980s it became apparent that companies with highly sophisticated CORPORATE PLANNING methods were not necessarily the most strategically successful. Competitors, often from abroad, seemed to be achieving global prominence without the formal, analytical approaches to corporate planning that many western companies used. Conventional assumptions about formal corporate planning came in for a reappraisal.

The crucial discovery, which had been known by military strategists for thousands of years, was that it is not possible to create strategies for an organisation until the strategies being pursued (and capable of being pursued) by rival (and potential rival) organisations are understood. Company-centred planning systems and the tools of professional corporate planning had failed to adopt this perspective. HELICOPTER VISION is needed to see the business in the context of its competitors and customers, and of the political, economic, social, and technological setting (see PEST). INDUSTRY ANALYSIS is needed.

Alternative strategies need to be developed, evaluated and, eventually, choices have to be made by the directors. Then the chosen strategies need supporting by appropriate POLICY-MAKING that lays down the guidelines for management. In formulating strategy and making related policy, a particular challenge to directors is to ensure that the long-term interests of the company are balanced with the short-term interests. Pressure to show strong performance in annual (even quarterly) directors' reports can all too easily adversely affect the pursuit of strategies that would fit the company for a better strategic future.

A significant trend in recent years has been away from strategies that emphasise business as a battlefield with global competitors and towards searching out strategic allies with whom mutually beneficial STRATEGIC ALLIANCES can be built. Major companies in the computer hardware industry, for example, have created hundreds of alliances with peripheral equipment manufacturers, software houses, and information service and entertainment providers.

In earlier days, when change and strategic challenge came relatively slowly, corporate planning was often an annual process, associated with the budget preparation. Today, strategy formulation, in most professionally led companies, is a constant activity for top management and the directors. Strategies tend to emerge as a stream of strategically significant information is digested and strategic options are discussed. Some boards of directors delegate much of the strategy formulation to the chief executive and top management. The outside directors act more as catalysts, probing the management's proposals, questioning their assumptions, challenging their conclusions, until a consensus is reached. Other boards are more closely involved in the details of strategic thinking. Recognising the importance of board-led strategic thinking, directors seem increasingly to be devoting specific board time and effort to strategy formulation, both during board meetings and by creating specific strategy sessions, often away from the boardroom.

In entrepreneurial firms strategies are often hidden and success often stems from unexpected and innovative strategies initiated by a dominant figure who has the ability to recognise strategic opportunities and seize them quickly. The boards of such companies are generally happy to give entrepreneurial business leaders the support they feel they need – at least for as long as the company continues its strategic success.

All men can see the tactics whereby I conquer: but none can see the strategy out of which victory is evolved.
Sun Tze, *The Art of War*, 6th century BC

The board of a large public corporation is an inappropriate body for developing strategy, setting corporate culture and policy and initiating major decisions. Instead the board should concentrate on the critical review of proposals, with management having the primary duty to formulate and then implement proposals.

The Hilmer Report, *Strictly Boardroom*, Australia, 1993

SUBOPTIMISATION

See GAMES DIRECTORS PLAY.

SUPERVISOR

One of the roles a director can play (see CONFORM-ANCE ROLES).

SUPERVISORY BOARD

The upper board in the TWO-TIER BOARD approach to CORPORATE GOVERNANCE. In the continental European model, the supervisory board monitors and supervises the performance of the executive board. Its power is derived from the ability to hire and fire the chief executive and other members of the executive. Joint membership of both the supervisory board and the executive board is not allowed. Some protagonists argue that the supervisory board distinguishes CONFORMANCE ROLES and PERFORMANCE ROLES that can become confused in a UNITARY BOARD. The critics of supervisory boards point out some of those that have failed, such as the Metallgesellschaft supervisory board, which was unable to detect the exposure to derivative trading in its US subsidiary, nearly causing the group to fail. (See *AUFSICHTSRAT* and *VORSTAND*.)

In designing systems of CORPORATE GOVERNANCE for state companies to be listed on overseas stock exchanges, the authorities in China adopted a unitary board (of executive and non-executive directors) to run the business plus a supervisory board to exercise oversight. (See CHINESE CORPORATE GOVERNANCE.)

SWOT ANALYSIS

A favourite analytical tool of CORPORATE PLANNING which involves taking a rigorous review of the Strengths and Weaknesses that the company has and the Opportunities and Threats that it faces. This technique is still used by many boards today. As a vehicle for focusing directors' attention on crucial strategic issues and building up their knowledge of the company's situation, SWOT analysis has value. Its fundamental weakness is that it is company-centred; that is the strategic thinkers are, as it were, sitting inside the company looking out. True strategic thinking requires the strategist to be able to perceive the company in the context of its industry, customers and competitors (see HELICOPTER VISION and STRATEGY FORMULATION).

TITLES

Not all people who carry the title of director are directors; and some who do not bear the title director may be held liable as though they were. Titles such as director of long range planning or director of private banking business may be useful to add status to the post, but do not necessarily imply membership of the board of directors. Such people would be ASSOCIATE DIRECTORS. On the other hand, SHADOW DIRECTORS are those who, while not formally having the title of director, influence board decisions. They may be held responsible, in law, for the exercise of that power.

TOKENISM

The inclusion of people on PUBLIC COMPANY boards of directors because they reflect (and can be seen to reflect) stakeholder interests such as consumers or gender, race or other minority concerns, rather than because of the specific contribution they can make to the board's work. Tokenism was at its height during the stakeholder debates of the 1970s, particularly among top US corporations. Today nomination committees that recommend women or members of other interest groups do so primarily because of their potential to contribute to the board's work, and not merely as a gesture to stakeholder groups.

TOMORROW'S COMPANY

A report from a group of UK business people, which argued that successful companies did not act solely for the benefit of shareholders but took an inclusive view of the interests of other stakeholders (without using that word), such as customers, suppliers and employees. (See HAMPEL REPORT for an alternative view.)

TWO HAT DILEMMA

The potential problem facing all executive directors: in the boardroom are they wearing the hat of a director responsible for the governance of the company as a whole, or are they wearing their executive hat and defending the management performance of their part of the organisation and representing its interests?

> *"I make it clear to all my executive directors that when they are in my board room they take off their executive hat and are responsible, with me, for the direction of the company as a whole."*
> Lord Caldecote, when chairman of the Delta Group

TWO-TIER BOARD

A governance structure found in continental European countries, such as Germany and the Netherlands, in which the executive board comprising the top executive team is entirely separate from the upper SUPERVISORY BOARD. (See also *AUFSICHTSRAT* and *VORSTAND*.)

> *The same reason which induced the Romans to have two consuls makes it desirable for there to be two chambers of parliament; that neither of them may be exposed to the corrupting influence of undivided power...*
> John Stewart Mill

U

UNITARY BOARD

Companies incorporated in the United States, the UK and other Commonwealth company law jurisdictions have boards with both executive and outside, non-executive directors. By contrast, companies incorporated in some continental European jurisdictions have a TWO-TIER BOARD. The unitary board can comprise entirely executive directors, have a minority or majority of outside, non-executive directors, or be composed entirely of non-executive directors.

VICE-CHAIR

A title used by some boards to spread the work-load of the chairman; by others to mark the chair-man-elect; and by yet others to confer prestige without necessarily giving additional responsibilities or powers (see CHAIR).

> *Chairman, Vice-chairman, President – the titles do not always mean quite what they seem. The man at the top of the pecking order may, indeed, be the big potato, but it is just as likely that he counts for nothing at all.*
> Robert Lacey, *Detroit's Destiny*

VIÉNOT REPORT

A report on corporate governance in France published in July 1995, which included the recommendation that "every board should set up an accounts or audit committee to ensure that the accounting methods used in preparing the accounts are pertinent and consistent … and should inform the AGM of its existence and the number of times it has met during the year".

VOLUNTARY ORGANISATIONS' GOVERNANCE

See NON-PROFIT DIRECTOR.

VORSTAND

The executive committee or board in the German TWO-TIER BOARD system of CORPORATE GOVERNANCE.

VOTING RIGHTS

The ARTICLES OF ASSOCIATION usually provide the terms and procedures for members' voting in general meetings of a company. If those attending a meeting vote by a show of hands, the size of individual shareholdings will not count; but if a poll is called for, the typical clause in the articles provides for one vote for each share. (See EQUITY and DUAL CLASS SHARE.)

VOTING WITH THEIR FEET

The tendency of some institutional investors to

prefer not to become involved in the governance issues of companies in which they have invested; in other words selling their shares rather than engaging in PROXY VOTING. (See also RELATIONSHIP INVESTOR.)

WAR ROOM

Some boards have their boardrooms fitted out with display screens and information-retrieval facilities to provide information pertinent to decisions under discussion. The analogy with the military operations room in a battle situation is, however, suspect since military operations involve real-time tactical responses as situations evolve, whereas the time horizon of board-level decisions should be long-term strategic.

WATCHDOG

A role a director can play (see CONFORMANCE ROLES.)

WINDOW-ON-THE-WORLD

A role a director can play (see PERFORMANCE ROLES.)

WISE MAN

A role a director can play (see PERFORMANCE ROLES.)

Women directors used to be in politics or good works: today they are younger, with relevant business experience.

Viki Holton, *Corporate Governance – an international review*,
Vol. 3, No. 2, April 1995

WOMAN DIRECTOR

Research has shown that more women are reaching the top levels of the major UK organisations; but a statistic that has remained constant is that just over 80% of women directors are non-executives. On current trends, it will not be before the year 2017 that there is at least one woman on the board of each of the *Times* Top 200 British companies.

WORKER DIRECTOR

See EMPLOYEE DIRECTOR.

WORKS COUNCIL

See EMPLOYEE DIRECTOR.

YAKUSA

Japanese gangster organisations, often run in a business-like, corporate manner. The *yakusa* sometimes threaten disruption of companies' AGMs if they are not suitably rewarded. These "general meeting fixers", as they are called in Japanese, are known as SOKAIYA. Consequently, many companies hold their AGMs on the same day. Links were found by a parliamentary committee in 1991 between a *yakusa* organisation and Nomura and Nikko securities companies, when it was alleged that they had helped the mobsters inflate the value of a railway company's stock for their own benefit.

ZAIBATSU

Closely related networks of Japanese companies which operated in the early years of the 20th century. After the second world war the occupying forces sought to disband the *zaibatsu* because of their previous close connections with military central powers. They were only partially successful and some of the *KEIRETSU* reflect the earlier relationships.

Part 3

APPENDICES

1 An induction checklist for directors

Outside directors never know enough about the business to be useful and inside directors always know too much to be independent. So runs one criticism of traditional board practice. Working through the items on this checklist will improve the quality of directors' contributions and reduce the time it takes for them to contribute fully and effectively. Induction exercises for directors will ensure that new board members are fully informed about the company, the business and its financials, the three fundamental areas in which directors need to be conversant and competent. Directors vary in the extent of their knowledge of the company and its business, but the checklist will provide an *aide memoire* for both outside and inside directors.

The checklist can be used by chairmen and CEOs planning an induction programme for their board members, as well as by newly appointed directors wanting to brief themselves. Many of the questions are ones they should ask before accepting a directorship. The checklist has also proved useful for directors of long standing, by highlighting areas of knowledge and work that they might previously have overlooked.

1 KNOWLEDGE OF THE COMPANY

The first broad focus of the induction programme is on the company and its governance. The chairman, other long-serving directors and the company secretary can often be very helpful in this regard. If in doubt, it is always wise to seek legal opinion.

Ownership power

In the joint stock limited liability company ownership is the ultimate basis of governance power. What is the balance of the equity shareholding and voting power? Has the balance changed in the past and how have the votes been used? How might it change and the voting strength be used in the future? Consider, in a family company, for example, what might happen as shares are transferred on succession. Or, in a widely held public company, consider the potential for a merger or hostile bid. What anti-takeover provisions, if any, are in place? How effective might they be?

In a company limited by guarantee, or any other corporate entity governed by its members, how active is the membership in governance matters? Could this situation change in the future? Explore the way that the board communicates with the members and whether there have been any attempts by members to influence corporate affairs. Non-profit organisations often seem to generate controversial, even adversarial, member activity.

Rules, regulations and company law
Study the articles of association and memorandum or corporate rule book. These are the formal documents created on incorporation and updated subject to the approval of the members. Within the constraints of the company law and the listing rules (for a quoted public company), they determine the way the company can be governed. The memorandum, for example, could limit the size of the board, lay down rules for the selection of the board chairman, or define conditions for the meeting and voting of the members. All too often directors are not familiar with the contents of the company's memorandum and are surprised to find themselves constrained in some way, for example, in the percentage of members' votes needed to change the capital structure or sell off part of the enterprise.

In a listed public company be familiar with the listing rules of the stock exchanges on which the company's shares are quoted. Some directors feel that this is a matter that can reasonably be left to the company secretary, share registrar or corporate legal counsel. But it is difficult for people not familiar with the basic requirements to ask appropriate questions that ensure compliance. There is an important distinction between delegation and abdication of responsibility.

Be familiar with the broad scope of the company law of the jurisdiction in which the company is incorporated and has its major bases. Obviously, the detailed requirements of company law vary between Delaware and California, Australia and Canada, or the UK and France, but there can also be fundamental differences, particularly in the handling of private companies. Companies incorporated in the British Virgin Islands, for example, are not required to have an audit, there is virtually no public filing of documents and the rights of members can be severely limited if they are not also directors.

It is not necessary for a director to be a lawyer or an accountant to fulfil such responsibilities, but company law around the world typically expects directors to show the degree of knowledge and skill that a reasonable person would associate with company directorship. In the old days this might not have amounted to very much; today expectations are running high.

Board structure, membership and processes

What is the structure of the board? In other words, what is the balance between executive and non-executive directors? In your opinion is this appropriate? Are the outside, non-executive directors independent, or do they have some connection with the company such as being a nominee for a major shareholder or lender, being members of the family of the chairman or CEO, or holding an executive directorship in the past? Such matters could affect your assessment of the position they take on board issues.

Is the board chairmanship separated from the role of chief executive? If not, is there a danger that the board is dominated by a single individual, and are you able to operate in such a climate? Who are the other board members? Do you know them? If not, some effort to learn about their background, experience and reputation could reinforce your early contributions to board discussions. Meeting individual directors to discuss corporate matters before your first board meeting might help you to discover whether the chemistry of the board is likely to be appropriate for you. Is there a succession plan for key directors and top management? Is there a strategy for development at board level to ensure that the business does not outgrow the board?

How often does the board meet? How long do typical meetings last? What role does the chairman play in board matters? Ask for the agenda and minutes of recent board meetings. Talk to the company secretary about the way the board meetings are run. Does the board operate with committees – an executive committee, audit, remuneration or nominating committees, for example? Find out what you can about the membership, chairmanship and style of these committees. Study their minutes and discuss with their chairman or the company secretary how they operate.

What information do the directors routinely receive? Ask for all the documentation provided for recent meetings. Study the reports and consider the scope of the routine performance data provided. Is it adequate? Does the board have briefings and presentations from non-board senior executives or other experts from time to time? Do the directors meet the auditors periodically?

2 KNOWLEDGE OF THE BUSINESS

The second focus of this induction checklist is on the business itself. Do you know enough about the business to make an effective contribution? This is a reasonable question to ask an outside director who has little or no experience in this particular industry. Interestingly, it is also a pertinent question to put to many executive directors. Expertise and success in a particular function (finance and accounting, perhaps) or high managerial performance in running a division or group company, does not necessarily provide a view of the business as a whole. Indeed, it might have created a narrow window of experience through which the entire corporate business is viewed. This part of the checklist is again relevant to all directors.

The basic business processes

Can you outline the fundamental steps in the added-value chain or network of the firm? This is as pertinent a question for directors of a bank, a telecommunications company or an airline, as it is for those of a manufacturing business (although the basic processes are often more difficult to identify). Are you familiar with the major sources of the business inputs, where they come from and who provides them? Within the business processes, which add the value and provide competitive advantage and which drive the costs? What are the core competences or capabilities of the business? What is the range of products and services provided by the business? Find out all you can from catalogues, trade literature, customer promotions, trade shows and similar sources of information. Who are the customers? What sectors and markets are served? Pareto's law often applies to products and customers: 80% of the value comes from 20% of the list. Which products and customers form this 20%?

Corporate strategies

Does the firm have a written mission statement or a set of core values? Is there a shared view of the business direction, clearly articulated in strategies, plans and projects? Obtain copies, discuss them with the chairman or CEO. If not, what is the broad direction of the business; what strategies are evident from recent actions, such as strategies of growth through investment in new product development or through acquisition and divestment? Are there any written policies or management manuals? Study and discuss them. For example, as far as customers are concerned, are there specific pricing policies and credit policies?

Who are the principal competitors? What competitive advantages and disadvantages do they have and what strategies are they pursuing? Are there potential entrants into the market or technological developments, products or services that might provide new competition? Is the business involved in strategic alliances; for example, joint ventures to develop new strategic areas, to supply goods or services, or provide access to distribution channels?

How is strategic change initiated in the firm? Does the board respond to ideas put forward by the CEO and top management, or is the board intimately involved in strategy formulation?

Organisation, management and people

What is the formal organisation structure? Discuss with the CEO and other members of top management how the organisation works in practice. Form a view of the management culture and style throughout the business: it may differ around the world.

What management control systems are used, such as budgetary planning and control, profit centres, performance centres and so on? What management performance measures are used? Are they linked to managerial incentives? Are there employee or top management share-option schemes?

How many employees are there in the various parts of the business? What are the characteristics of the workforce? Are trade unions important and is there a policy towards them? What are the remuneration and other employment policies?

Overall, how would you assess the current position of the business? What needs to be done to maintain and enhance future performance?

3 KNOWLEDGE OF THE FINANCIALS

Finally, we turn to a sector which inevitably features strongly in typical board discussions: the financial aspects.

Study the annual accounts and directors' reports for the past few years. What have been the trends?

Consider the trends of key financial ratios, for

example: overall performance ratios, such as return on equity and return on investment; and working capital management ratios, such as inventory turnover rates, liquidity ratios, debt collection rates. Does the company measure shareholder added-value?

Trends are likely to convey more information than the actual ratios for the business itself, whereas the financial ratios at a point in time can be useful for cross-industry comparisons. What are the future projections for these financial criteria? How does the financial position of the company compare with that of its key competitors?

Review the financial performance of parts of the business, such as product or geographical divisions or subsidiary companies. Review the criteria used in investment project appraisals.

How is the company financed? What is the financial structure? What implications might the debt:equity ratio have for the future? For example, what might be the effect of a significant change in interest rates given this gearing or leverage?

Who are the auditors? Ask to see the "management letter" written after the last audit discussing any issues that arose during the audit.

4 EXPECTATIONS ON APPOINTMENT

All directors should discuss with the chairman what is expected of their directorship before accepting nomination. Consequently, a crucial part of any induction briefing should review the expectations of the chairman and the other directors.

Is a specific role expected of you? Was there a special reason, perhaps, why you were nominated for the board? For example, did the nomination reflect your particular knowledge in some area, or that you would bring special skills or experience to board discussions, or provide a special channel of communication and information? Or was the nomination made because of your overall experience and potential contribution to all aspects of the board's work? Are you capable of fulfilling these expectations? If not, what other information, knowledge, skill will you need to obtain?

How much time are you expected to give to the board, its committees and to other aspects of the company's affairs? This should cover not only attendance at regular meetings, but also the time needed for briefings and discussions, visits within the company and preparation. Outside directors will have to ensure that this is compatible with other demands on their time. Executive directors will need to harmonise these expectations and their director responsibilities with the duties required under their contracts of employment with the company.

Although all directors have the right to be informed on all board matters, confirm that you will have appropriate access to the information you require. This should cover not only formal board papers, but also the right to seek additional information if necessary. Are you able to talk to the members of management? If so, under what circumstances?

Last, but not least, review the details of the contractual relationship between you and the company. Is there a written contract or a formal letter of appointment from the chairman? What are the terms of appointment as a director? Length of appointment? Terms and likelihood of reappointment? Basis of the remuneration package and manner of review? Terms of any director and officers' indemnity insurance (particularly important in the increasingly litigious climate in which directors in many parts of the world have to operate)?

Finally, a word of encouragement. All directors, without exception, face a challenge as they join a new board. Effective board membership involves a learning experience. It should start well before the director attends the first board meeting and should continue during all the rest. The successful director is the one who can say: "Aha! I hadn't realised that, now I understand," not once but continuously, throughout his or her service to the board.

2 Director core competencies: the MTRC case study

The Mass Transit Railway Corporation (MTRC) operates the subway system in Hong Kong, including the line to the new airport, and manages the related residential, office and shopping complexes. The MTRC carries more passengers each year than the London Transport Underground system, which has ten times the length of track.

The corporation is managed by a team of executive directors led by the chairman. The present chairman, like his two predecessors, fills the role of both chairman and managing director. Main board members are government appointees, with only the chairman/managing director being executive, although it is normal practice for the executive directors to be present at board meetings.

When the board of the MTRC approved the implementation of a corporate-wide management assessment process, they recognised that succession planning and development at executive director level was a priority. Two crucial questions emerged: was it possible to identify the core competencies that are required by directors? If so, could those competencies be measured and assessed objectively? The experiences of the MTRC in identifying director competencies and in designing, validating and implementing the assessment process suggests that they can. Their experience forms the basis of this case.

The full text of this case, with material on assessment centres, can be found in Tricker, R. I., and Kelly Lee. "Assessing Directors' Core Competencies", *Corporate Governance – an international review*, Vol. 5, No. 2, April 1997. The innovative work of the MTRC in applying assessment centre methodologies to director-level activities is recognised; and the support of the chairman and senior management of the MTRC in permitting publication of the case research on their experiences is gratefully acknowledged.

The core competencies of company directors

What competencies should people have if they are to perform effectively as company directors? This beguilingly straightforward question, as yet, lacks a straightforward answer.

Neither the legal literature nor the common law provides an answer to the question of what core competencies are necessary for effective company direction. The descriptive and anecdotal literature of corporate governance lays great store on board structures, membership and procedures, emphasising the importance of interpersonal skills if directors are to interact effectively, and of the need for directors to have the moral fibre to take tough-minded decisions with the necessary gravitas, supplemented by an appropriate modicum of business knowledge and experience. Official reports on corporate governance have called for good governance practices through appropriate board structures, the use of board committees and disclosure, but they do not mention the roles of individual directors or the competencies needed to fulfil them adequately. Little serious research has been done on defining, measuring and refining such core competencies.

In 1993/94 the UK Institute of Directors, sponsored by the Department of Employment, launched an initiative to explore what made for good practice at board level. Henley Management College was commissioned to undertake the research. Insights into perceptions of good board-level practice were obtained through interviews with individual practising directors, focus groups of directors and detailed questionnaires sent to directors and others whose opinions could be significant. The results "represented a comprehensive view of good practice drawn from a very broad cross section of commercial companies in diverse settings ... covering a greatly varied spectrum of corporate size and type, encompassing small firms, private and public companies, and subsidiaries of both UK and foreign-owned companies." (Institute of Directors, 1995.) Subsequently, the Institute of Directors developed a set of standards for good board practice, based on the findings of the Henley research.

The MTRC executive director competencies

In the MTRC project director core competencies were defined as those critical to success as a director of that company. The competencies did not attempt to describe all that is required to carry out the role, rather they attempted to identify the high-level discriminators for success as a director. In other words, anyone aspiring to become a director should be able to align their aspirations and concentrate their development efforts against the required attributes for success. Further, by measuring individuals against these criteria, the organisation could establish the "fit" between the competencies of potential successors and those needed to be successful as executive directors.

The competencies were derived from an in-depth job analysis study using three separate job analysis techniques.

1 Expert, international input on directors' responsibilities both explicit and implicit, as well as legal requirements and current trends in the area of corporate governance.

2 An in-depth analysis of the papers tabled at meetings of the executive directors over a six-month period, to determine the scope of the directors' work.

3 Structured interviews with the current directors and the chairman.

The core-competencies that the MTRC identified are listed below.

Strategic vision and planning
The ability to think independently, originally and proactively; to take a broad cross-functional corporate view; to have vision for the future; to be capable of taking into account and foresee the implications of important economic, social and political developments; to be able to identify both strategic direction for the corporation and develop

broad comprehensive strategies for introducing change or preventing recurrences of problems which are clearly capable of being translated into management action.

Strategic reasoning skills
To be capable of synthesising and integrating information from a number of sources and establish hypotheses, theories or a more complete body of related information; to possess strong powers of analysis, capable of quickly reading and accurately interpreting large volumes of often technically complex information and data; the ability to apply principles of logic to solve both conceptual and practical problems; to have highly developed critical faculties, capable of objectively discriminating the relative priorities of strategic issues.

Decision-making
The ability to exercise judgment bringing to bear all relevant information to arrive at decisions often involving the allocation of fiscal resources; to be capable of deciding action through consensus with others and of taking tough commercially necessary decisions as well as difficult decisions affecting the welfare of others; the ability to evaluate information objectively and pragmatically and draw sound logical conclusions even when under pressure and on occasion extreme time constraints.

Team membership and directing skills
The ability to work effectively and flexibly as a member of a peer group team, taking charge of the team in crisis where his/her technical expertise is required, while at the same time being capable of deferring to other team members as more appropriate leaders in other situations and giving them full support; to provide strategic direction for others and to delegate and empower management to implement appropriate action; to act as an objective overseer of management performance and decisions.

Communication skills
The ability to express ideas clearly and persuasively to both internal and external bodies; to be capable of listening carefully and acting as a sounding board for the chairman and other directors; the personality predisposition to be culturally sensitive and capable of creating empathy with a wide range of diverse people; to be a strong negotiator able to remain calm and controlled in often emotional situations and under aggressive questioning; to have good formal presentation skills.

Personal strength and motivation
To have high personal integrity and strong motivation for achievement; to be prepared to stand one's ground; to have the courage of one's convictions and yet at the same time also prepared to reach reasonable compromise; not to be unreasonably stubborn but persistent; not to give in to difficulties and be dedicated to completing tasks whatever the time or effort required; to be loyal to the corporation and prepared to put the organisation ahead of personal preferences.

Political awareness and networking skills
The ability to initiate and maintain a wide range of contacts in government and political circles; to keep up professional contact; to be capable of commanding respect in the international community; to be diplomatic and demonstrate good social skills; to be politically astute, skilful at lobbying support internally and externally and capable of persuading and influencing individuals of equal or greater status and power.

Professional corporate and commercial understanding
To keep up-to-date with and be able to command professional respect within own field of expertise; to have a good understanding of the workings of the corporation as well as a sound grasp of developments in the transport industry worldwide; to be customer oriented as well as concerned with getting a good deal for the corporation, alert to commercial opportunities, and sensitive to market

movements; to have a good understanding of financial management and the operations of international money markets.

Assessing director core competencies

If director competencies can be identified in specific corporate situations, can assessment exercises, a process often referred to as assessment centres, be developed to measure them?

Assessment centres, employing multiple assessment methods, have been growing in popularity throughout the world as a means of looking at an individual's strengths, limitations and development needs in a thorough and reliable manner.

Despite the widespread use of the term "assessment centre", most authorities agree that, in fact, the phrase refers to a set of activities rather than a physical place: a process rather than a location. Typically, an assessment centre involves a series of activities designed to assess the suitability of candidates for a particular function or appointment, using a number of different measurement techniques in an environment removed from their day-to-day workplace. A major drawback of assessment centres is their cost. They are expensive to set up and very demanding of the time of the skilled observers and participants.

The MTRC assessment centre for executive directors

The company identified four specific objectives for the assessment centre exercise.

1 To identify executive director potential, as the basis for succession planning.
2 To create personal development plans.
3 To provide the basis for targeted and specific training and development.
4 To provide a realistic picture of opportunities for executives to take career decisions.

The assessment centre exercises were run in-house, with the help of consultants with expertise in various fields, including psychometric testing, experience in designing, validating and using assessment exercises and in director-level work and corporate governance. The consultants provided guidance in defining the core competencies, in designing the activities of the assessment centre and acted as observers in some of the assessment exercises.

Eight exercises were developed for the MTRC assessment centre. Each exercise was designed to assess more than one competence and the matrix in Figure 12 shows which exercises were used to assess which competencies. The results from each exercise were fed back to the observers in a concluding integration session, at which the performance of each participant was discussed at length and the final assessment made.

Eighteen participants, drawn from the echelon of top management immediately below executive director level, took part in each assessment centre. Some of the exercises involved individual work, others group work. Participants were divided into three groups of six. Six observers were involved in each assessment centre: three experienced external consultants and three of the existing executive directors. All had specific training for this assessment centre so that they were familiar with the exercises, and all were skilled in observing and recording behaviour to ensure a fair and objective assessment of each participant.

The MTRC executive director assessment centre used five exercises specifically designed to test the core competencies and three psychometric instruments. These were as follows.

The written strategy paper

A case study was prepared specifically for the assessment exercise. The simulated situation was one in which the chairman of the company had called for a written brief in three hours advising him on the response to make to a merger proposal As shown in the matrix in Figure 12, this exercise was designed to assess four competencies: strategic reasoning skills; strategic vision and planning; professional, corporate and commercial understanding; and decision-making abilities.

The analysis presentation

This used a proprietary exercise in which each participant was provided with material about the business affairs of a simulated travel agency. The information included data about the company history, current operations including products, market shares, turnover, profitability, premises, information technology, sales and marketing, human resources, head office administration, finances and current strategies being pursued. The information was complex and, as far as possible, true to life. Participants had 75 minutes to study this material and make notes. Each participant was then called on to make a 15 minute presentation to two assessors, synthesising the situation facing the company, suggesting comprehensive strategies from a broad cross-functional perspective, exercising judgments to reach those conclusions and presenting their views clearly, persuasively and succinctly.

The strategic discussion

This exercise, which was designed specifically for the MTRC assessment centre, was designed to assess participants' behaviour in meetings and to see how effective they were when working in a board-level team.

The media interview

Each participant was interviewed on camera by an experienced TV interviewer from one of the Hong Kong television stations. Half an hour beforehand the participants received a brief about the possible areas of questioning, which included some material about public issues facing the company.

The self-report

Prepared specifically for the MTRC assessment centre, the self-report form contained six pages on which each participant was asked to provide evidence on their performance on the core competencies of strategic vision and planning, professional, corporate and commercial under-standing, political awareness and networking skills, strategic reasoning.

The motivation questionnaire

This was a proprietary psychometric test, involv-ing a self-reporting inventory. Respondents were asked to rate 144 statements on how each one might affect their motivation at work. The results were mapped on to a profile sheet grouped into four categories: energy and dynamism; synergy; intrinsic motivation; and extrinsic motivation.

Test of Productive Thinking (TPT)

The second proprietary psychometric test con-sisted of a number of different occupational prob-lems in which the respondent was asked either to give as many explanations as possible as to why the problem occurred or to suggest as many solu-tions to the problem as possible.

Occupational Personality Questionnaire (OPQ)

The third proprietary psychometric test consisted of a self-report in which the respondents selected from four work-related activities which ones were most typical and least typical of their behaviour. The results were mapped against a profile of char-acteristics grouped into the three categories: rela-tionships; thinking style; feelings and emotions.

Rating participants

After every exercise each observer completed a rating form for the participants they had been observing. Ratings were made against the criteria being assessed on the matrix (Figure 12), using a seven-point assessment scale from excellent to poor in terms of potential to operate at executive director level.

Integration session

At the conclusion of the assessment centre, once all the ratings had been collated and computerised summaries produced, all the assessors gathered for an integration session. The purpose was to

Figure 12 MTRC Executive Directors Assessment Centre

	Written strategy paper	*Analysis presentation*	*Strategic discussion*
Professional corporate and commercial understanding	✔✔		
Political awareness and networking skills			✔
Team membership and directing skills			✔✔
Strategic vision and planning	✔✔	✔✔	
Strategic reasoning skills	✔✔	✔	
Decision-making	✔	✔✔	✔
Communication skills		✔	✔
Personal strength and motivation			✔

✔ the exercise contributes some information on this competence

	Media interview	Self-report	Motivation questionnaire	TPT	OPQ
Matrix of exercises used to assess specific competencies					
	✔	✔			✔
	✔	✔✔	✔		✔
			✔		✔
		✔		✔	✔
		✔		✔	✔
					✔
	✔✔				✔
	✔	✔	✔✔		✔

✔✔ the exercise provides primary information on this competence ensure that each participant was fairly and objectively assessed. A matrix of ratings, mirroring the competencies and exercises in Figure 12, was drawn up for each candidate. The ratings that the assessors had assigned to that candidate's performance in each exercise were discussed and an overall rating agreed.

Summary report and feedback to participants

After the assessment centre, each observer was required to write final reports on the two of the participants. These summary reports were intended to reflect the overall, considered opinions derived in the integration session, reflecting the views of all the observers. Feedback to participants was a vital part of the assessment process. This meets the moral commitment between company and participant to ensure fairness, prevent distortion and provide the motivation that comes from being able to discuss the process and its findings.

Overall results

The assessment centre results enabled participants to be grouped into people with high potential, that is those able to assume the role of executive director immediately; people of medium potential able to take up the role within about two years given appropriate development; those with long-term potential given appropriate development and experience; and those who demonstrated no potential to operate as executive directors.

The assessment enabled succession plans to be made in the light of the corporation's needs, including expected retirements and the possibility of new executive director posts being created. It also facilitated the creation of training and career development activities for each individual.

One of the executive directors who participated in the assessment process commented on the outcome that some people who had already shown significant managerial ability as functional heads did not show up so well on their executive director competencies, and some people who were assessed highly on these competencies had not shown up particularly well on a previous assessment centre for senior management abilities. This reinforces the view that managerial and governance competencies are different and distinguishable. The evidence of the MTRC experience suggests that the core competencies required by executive directors can be identified and objectively assessed.

3 A board effectiveness checklist

There is no board of directors or governing body in the world which, if the members think about it, cannot improve its effectiveness. This is the belief behind this checklist of opportunities. All too readily board members grow old together. Often the business outgrows the board. Few boards take a rigorous look at themselves. A review of board effectiveness can be a salutary experience, but it can lead to important changes.

A board review involves a comprehensive and tough-minded look at the board and its activities. The aim is to explore the board's structure, style and processes in the light of changing company needs, to highlight potential problems for the future and provide the basis for improving effectiveness today.

Such a review needs the enthusiastic support and co-operation of all board members if it is to succeed. It can be led by the chairman, one of the outside directors, an *ad hoc* board committee or someone with suitable experience from outside the board. It is obviously a highly confidential activity.

The review process involves marshalling a lot of information about the underlying governance power-base in the company, the board structure and its members, and the way the board and its committees work, including the information they receive and the way they allocate their time. Various ideas, issues and opinions will then emerge. Alternatives can be developed and evaluated. In due course the options can be discussed by the directors, leading eventually to a strategy for the development of the board and the way it works. The process needs to be taken step by step.

1 Set the board review in the context of the company's business strategy

As companies grow in complexity, diversity and size, it seems obvious that their boards ought also to evolve to reflect such changes. Unfortunately this is not always the case. If, for example, the company's strategy involves new technologies, markets or international locations, if it is developing new strategic alliance or acquisition strategies, or if its plans call for alternative global financing strategies such as the use of derivatives, it is essential that among the board members are those able to understand the issues and, in due course, monitor executive management's performance. Thus the first step towards creating a strategy for board development is to consider the implications at board level of the corporate business strategy as a whole. The board review must be in line with, and preferably part of, the company's overall business strategy.

2 Review overall governance

This can be particularly important, yet easily overlooked. The key question is: who has ultimate power over the company and might this change over the strategic time horizon of the board review? If so, what would be the implications for governance and the board? For example, in a public listed company what are the prospects of a change of ownership through a friendly or hostile bid? Or in a company with a dominant shareholder, what might happen to the board if this shareholding changed hands? In a family firm, how might the balance of power change on succession? It is important not only to know precisely the current ownership of the voting equity, but also to consider possible future scenarios. Detailed knowledge of the company's articles of association is important as well. There may be unexpected clauses about percentages of shareholder votes needed to approve various strategic changes, such as introducing new capital or divesting part of the business.

3 Consider relevant external factors

This means looking at the context in which the governance of the company must operate over the time horizon of the review. Are there any legal, political or societal factors that could affect the governance of the company? Examples include possible changes to company legislation in any of the countries in which the company operates, new regulations from the European Union about worker representation in strategic decision-making, the imposition of new disclosure requirements in the stock exchange listing rules, or the possible effects of a change of government. Any plans for developing the board must take account of the changing governance environment.

4 Review board structure

Consider the size of the board. Is it appropriate for the task that needs to be done? There may be a case for additional members; on the other hand, the board may have grown too big. Consider the structure of the board. Is the balance between executive and non-executive members appropriate? This issue will have to be reviewed along with the identification of board style and the way the members work together. Are enough of the non-executive directors genuinely independent? This means ensuring that the independent outside directors have no relationships with the company that could affect the exercise of genuinely objective judgment. Are the posts of chairman of the board and chief executive separate? Is the present arrangement the most satisfactory for the future?

5 Identify board style

Consider how the board's work has evolved in recent years. Reflect on the effects of changes in chairman and other members. Review the way the directors work together. Is this a genuinely professional board style or are there elements of the rubber stamp, the representative board or the country club? What changes might be necessary to meet different circumstances that may arise in the future?

6 Review board membership and the roles directors play; formulate succession plans

Consider the detailed membership of the board. Summarise the resume of each director. Does the board have the balance of knowledge, skills and experience that will be needed for the planned future of the company? Categorise the roles that directors play on the board. Is the balance appropriate now and in the future? Look at the age profile of members. How many directors will retire over the review's time horizon? What is the probability of any directors resigning? Develop succession plans for both executive and non-executive directors. Boards should always have a portfolio of potential non-executive directors who could be considered for board appointment, and the management development plans for senior executive staff should also include their potential as directors. (See Director core competencies: the MTRC case in Appendix 2.)

7 Consider director development and training

As much attention should be given to director development and training as is given to management development and training, but it seldom is. Directors all too readily assume that, having reached the board, they must have the experience to perform as directors. But governance, the work of the board, is not the same as management. It calls for additional knowledge and different skills. Consider the development needs of each director. This could involve a carefully devised induction or updating programme on the company and its work; or building up experience by, for example, chairing a board task force or one of the board committees; or it might be achieved through participation in the growing number of director-level courses and programmes around the world.

8 Achieving greater efficiency: review directors' time and information

How does the board spend its time? Is this the most effective use of one of the most valuable resources the company has? Does the board delegate some of its work to board committees and are these as effective as they could be? This information can be extracted from an analysis of the agenda and minutes of the board and its committees, and by discussing the issue with each director. Similarly, review the nature, extent and adequacy of the information available to directors. How could the routine board papers be improved? Can directors readily obtain the additional information they want? Do the outside directors have access to management information? Is there a case for board-level briefings to keep directors up to date and provide the context for board-level discussions? What ideas does each director have for improvement in the information process?

9 Achieving greater effectiveness: better strategy formulation and policy-making

Review the board's contribution to the performance roles of strategy formulation and policy-making. Is adequate time devoted to this part of the board's responsibilities? Are all board members adequately informed about strategic matters? Is there a shared vision and understanding of the company's core values and competences among all the directors? Are there any differences of view as to the strategic direction of the firm? Are the policy guidelines laid down by the board adequate for management decision-making, balancing control and freedom appropriately? What ideas do directors have for improvement?

10 Achieving greater effectiveness: better executive supervision and accountability

Turning to the conformance roles of the board, do the directors adequately monitor and supervise executive management? Is the feedback of information relevant and timely? How might the process be improved? Seek the opinions of all directors and senior managers, also the auditors and others in a position to take a view on board activities. Is the board providing appropriate accountability to all those with a legitimate claim to be informed? Does this include a commitment to employees, customers and suppliers, or does the board accept a responsibility to be accountable only to the shareholders? Is this responsibility adequately fulfilled? Consider the published report, other communications and meetings with the members, analysts and the media. What ideas are there for improvement?

11 Develop and agree the strategy for board development

From the mass of hard data, opinion and ideas for improvement that have been gathered, marshal the facts, identify alternatives and articulate their implications. Develop a report for discussion by the board. To encourage open discussion and creativity such a review might well take place as part of a strategy seminar, rather than in a formal board meeting. Move towards developing a strategy for developing the board. This could include planned changes to board size, structure or membership, new sources and forms of providing information, alternative uses of directors' time (such as a new committee structure), alternative formats for board meetings, or calling on some directors to commit different amounts of time to their board duties. Agree the strategy, ensuring that it is consistent with, indeed part of, the overall business strategy.

12 Determine action plans and projects

Finally, develop the procedures, plans and projects that will turn the strategy into realised change. Ensure commitment from all those involved. Get feedback periodically to confirm that the changes are taking place as planned and that the results are as expected. Continue the strategic review and programme for change as part of the board's constant learning and relearning process.

4 Principles of good governance and code of best practice

The Hampel Report (1998) proposed that the principles and codes of the Cadbury Report (1992) and the Greenbury Report (1995) should be combined. The Hampel Committee passed the proposed combined code to the London Stock Exchange which published it as a consultation document in March 1998. The changes to the original codes were minor.

The Hampel Committee envisaged that, after a period of consultation, the London Stock Exchange would amend the Listing Rules to require listed companies to make a disclosure statement in two parts. The first part would report on how companies had applied the principles. The Hampel Report made clear it did not prescribe the form or content of this part of the statement, the intention being that companies should have a free hand to explain their governance policies in the light of the principles, including any special circumstances applying to them which had led to a particular approach. In the second part of the statement the company would be required either to confirm that it complies with the code provisions or, where it does not, provide an explanation. It must be for the shareholders and others to evaluate such explanations.

PART 1 – PRINCIPLES

Section 1 – Companies

A Directors
I   *The board.* Every listed company should be headed by an effective board which should lead and control the company.

II   *Chairman and CEO.* There are two key tasks at the top of every public company – the running of the board and the executive responsibility for the running of the company's business. There should be a clearly accepted division of responsibilities at the head of the company, which will ensure a balance of power and authority, such that no one individual has unfettered powers of decision.

III *Board balance.* The board should include a balance of executive and non-executive directors (including independent non-executives) such that no individual or small group of individuals can dominate the board's decision taking.

IV *Supply of information.* The board should be supplied in a timely manner with information in a form and of a quality appropriate to enable it to discharge its duties.

V *Appointments to the board.* There should be a formal and transparent procedure for the appointment of new directors to the board.

VI *Re-election.* All directors should be required to submit themselves for re-election at regular intervals and at least every three years.

B Directors' remuneration

I *The level and make-up of remuneration.* Levels of remuneration should be sufficient to attract and retain the directors needed to run the company successfully. The component parts of executive directors' remuneration should be structured so as to link rewards to corporate and individual performance.

II *Procedure.* Companies should establish a formal and transparent procedure for developing policy on executive remuneration and for fixing the remuneration packages of individual directors. No director should be involved in fixing his or her own remuneration.

III *Disclosure.* The company's annual report should contain a statement of remuneration policy and details of the remuneration of each director.

C Relations with shareholders

I *Dialogue with institutional shareholders.* Companies should be ready, where practicable, to enter into a dialogue with institutional

shareholders based on the mutual
understanding of objectives.

II   *Constructive use of the AGM*. Companies should
use the AGM to communicate with private
investors and encourage their participation.

D   Accountability and audit

I   *Financial reporting*. The board should present a
balanced and understandable assessment of the
company's position and prospects.

II   *Internal control*. The board should maintain a
sound system of internal control to safeguard
shareholders' investment and the company's
assets.

III   *Relationship with the auditors*. The board
should establish formal and transparent
arrangements for considering how they should
apply the financial reporting and internal
control principles and for maintaining an
appropriate relationship with the company's
auditors.

Section 2 – Institutional shareholders

I   *Shareholder voting*. Institutional shareholders
have a responsibility to make considered use of
their votes.

II   *Dialogue with companies*. Institutional
shareholders should be ready, where
practicable, to enter into a dialogue with
companies based on the mutual understanding
of objectives.

III   *Evaluation of governance disclosures*. When
evaluating companies' governance
arrangements, particularly those relating to
board structure and composition, institutional
investors should give due weight to all relevant
factors drawn to their attention.

PART 2 – CODE

Section 1 – Companies

A   Directors

Principle
The board. Every listed company should be headed by an effective board which should lead and control the company.

Code provisions
A.1   The board should meet regularly.

A.2   The board should have a formal schedule of matters specifically reserved to it for decision.

A.3   There should be an agreed procedure for directors in the furtherance of their duties to take independent professional advice if necessary, at the company's expense.

A.4   All directors should have access to the advice and services of the company secretary, who is responsible to the board for ensuring that board procedures are followed and that applicable rules and regulations are complied with. Any question of the removal of the company secretary should be a matter for the board as a whole.

A.5   All directors should bring an independent judgment to bear on issues of strategy, performance, resources, including key appointments, and standards of conduct.

A.6   An individual should receive appropriate training on the first occasion that he or she is appointed to the board of a listed company, and subsequently as necessary.

Principle
Chairman and CEO. There are two key tasks at the top of every public company – the running of the board and the executive responsibility for the running of the company's business. There should be a clearly accepted division of responsibilities at the head of the company which will ensure a balance of power and authority, such that no one individual has unfettered powers of decision.

Code provision

A.7 A decision to combine the posts of chairman and chief executive officer in one person should be publicly explained. Whether the posts are held by different people or by the same person, there should be a strong and independent non-executive element on the board, with a recognised senior member other than the chairman. The chairman, chief executive and senior independent director should be identified in the annual report.

Principle

Board balance. The board should include a balance of executive and non-executive directors (including independent non-executives) such that no individual or small group of individuals can dominate the board's decision taking.

Code provisions

A.8 The board should include non-executive directors of sufficient calibre and number for their views to carry significant weight in the board's decisions. Non-executive directors should comprise not less than one-third of the board.

A.9 The majority of non-executive directors should be independent of management and free from any business or other relationship which could materially interfere with the exercise of their independent judgement. Non-executive directors considered by the board to be independent should be identified in the annual report.

Principle

Supply of information. The board should be supplied in a timely manner with information in a form and of a quality appropriate to enable it to discharge its duties.

Code provision

A.10 Management has an obligation to provide the board with appropriate and timely information, but information volunteered by management is unlikely to be enough in all circumstances and directors should make further enquiries where necessary. The chairman should ensure that all directors are properly briefed on issues arising at board meetings.

Principle

Appointments to the board. There should be a formal and transparent procedure for the appointment of new directors to the board.

Code provision

A. 11   Unless the board is small, a nomination committee should be established to make recommendations to the board on all new board appointments. A majority of the members of this committee should be non-executive directors, and the chairman should be either the chairman of the board or a non-executive director. The chairman and members of the nomination committee should be identified in the annual report.

Principle

Re-election. All directors should be required to submit themselves for re-election at regular intervals and at least every three years.

Code provision

A.12   Non-executive directors should be appointed for specified terms and reappointment should not be automatic. All directors should be subject to election by shareholders at the first opportunity after their appointment, and to re-election thereafter at intervals of no more than three years. The names of directors submitted for election or re-election should be accompanied by full biographical details.

B   Directors' remuneration

Principle

The level and make-up of remuneration. Levels of

remuneration should be sufficient to attract and retain the directors needed to run the company successfully. The component parts of executive directors' remuneration should be structured so as to link rewards to corporate and individual performance.

Code provisions

Remuneration policy

B.1 Remuneration committees should provide the packages needed to attract, retain and motivate executive directors of the quality required but should avoid paying more than is necessary for this purpose.

B.2 Remuneration committees should judge where to position their company relative to other companies. They should be aware what comparable companies are paying and should take account of relative performance. But they should use such comparisons with caution, in view of the risk that they can result in an upward ratchet of remuneration levels with no corresponding improvement in performance.

B.3 Remuneration committees should be sensitive to the wider scene, including pay and employment conditions elsewhere in the group, especially when determining annual salary increases.

B.4 The performance-related elements of remuneration should form a significant proportion of the total remuneration package of executive directors and should be designed to align their interests with those of shareholders and to give these directors keen incentives to perform at the highest levels.

B.5 Executive share options should never be offered at a discount.

B.6 In designing schemes of performance related remuneration, remuneration committees should follow the provisions in Schedule A to this code.

Service contracts and compensation

B.7 There is a strong case for setting notice or contract periods at, or reducing them to, one year or less. Boards should set this as an objective; but they should recognise that it may not be possible to achieve it immediately.

B.8 If it is necessary to offer longer notice or contract periods to new directors recruited from outside, such periods should reduce after the initial period.

B.9 Remuneration committees should consider what compensation commitments (including pension contributions) their directors' contracts of service, if any, would entail in the event of early termination. They should in particular consider the advantages of providing explicitly in the initial contract for such compensation commitments except in the case of removal for misconduct.

B.10 Where the initial contract does not explicitly provide for compensation commitments, remuneration committees should, within legal constraints, tailor their approach in individual early termination cases to the wide variety of circumstances. The broad aim should be to avoid rewarding poor performance while dealing fairly with cases where departure is not due to poor performance and to take a robust line on reducing compensation to reflect departing directors' obligations to mitigate damages.

Principle

Procedure. Companies should establish a formal and transparent procedure for developing policy on executive remuneration and for fixing the remuneration packages of individual directors. No director should be involved in fixing his or her own remuneration.

Code provisions

B.11 To avoid potential conflicts of interest, boards of directors should set up remuneration committees of independent non-executive directors to make recommendations to the board, within agreed terms of reference, on the company's framework of executive remuneration and its cost; and to determine on their behalf specific remuneration packages for each of the executive directors, including pension rights and any compensation payments.

B.12 Remuneration committees should consist exclusively of independent non-executive directors with no personal financial interest other than as shareholders in the matters to be decided, no potential conflicts of interest arising from cross-directorships and no day-to-day involvement in running the business.

B.13 The members of the remuneration committee should be listed each year in the board's remuneration report to shareholders (B.17 below).

B.14 The board itself or, where required by the Articles of Association, the shareholders should determine the remuneration of the non-executive directors, including members of the remuneration committee, within the limits set in the Articles of Association. Where permitted by the Articles, the board may however delegate this responsibility, case by case, to a small subcommittee, which might include the chief executive officer.

B.15 Remuneration committees should consult the chairman and/or chief executive officer about their proposals relating to the remuneration of other executive directors and have access to professional advice inside and outside the company.

B.16 The chairman of the board should ensure that the company maintains contact as required with its principal shareholders about remuneration in the same way as for other matters.

Principle
Disclosure. The company's annual report should contain a statement of remuneration policy and details of the remuneration of each director.

Code provisions
B.17 The board should report to the shareholders each year on remuneration. The report should form part of, or be annexed to, the company's

annual report and accounts. It should be the main vehicle through which the company accounts to shareholders for directors' remuneration.

B.18 The report should set out the company's policy on executive directors' remuneration. It should draw attention to factors specific to the company.

B.19 In preparing the remuneration report, the board should follow the provisions in Schedule B to this code.

B.20 Shareholders should be invited specifically to approve all new long-term incentive schemes (including share option schemes) whether payable in cash or shares in which directors and senior executives will participate which potentially commit shareholders' funds over more than one year or dilute the equity.

B.21 The board's annual remuneration report to shareholders need not be a standard item of agenda for AGMs. But the board should consider each year whether the circumstances are such that the AGM should be invited to approve the policy set out in the report and should minute their conclusions.

C Relations with shareholders

Principle
Dialogue with institutional shareholders. Companies should be ready, where practicable, to enter into a dialogue with institutional shareholders based on the mutual understanding of objectives.

Principle
Constructive use of the AGM. Companies should use the AGM to communicate with private investors and encourage their participation.

Code provisions
C. 1 Companies should count all proxy votes and announce the proxy count on each resolution after it has been dealt with on a show of hands.

C.2 Companies should propose a separate

resolution at the AGM on each substantially separate issue, and should in particular propose a resolution at the AGM relating to the report and accounts.

C.3 The chairman of the board should arrange for the chairmen of the audit, remuneration and nomination committees to be available to answer questions at the AGM.

C.4 Companies should arrange for the Notice of the AGM and related papers to be sent to shareholders at least 20 working days before the meeting.

D   Accountability and audit

Principle
Financial reporting. The board should present a balanced and understandable assessment of the company's position and prospects.

Code provision
D. 1 The directors should explain their responsibility for preparing the accounts, next to a statement by the auditors about their reporting responsibilities.

D.2 The board should consider interim and other price-sensitive public reports and reports to regulators as well as information required to be presented by statutory requirements.

Principle
Internal control. The board should maintain a sound system of internal control to safeguard shareholders' investment and the company's assets.

Code provisions
D.3 The directors should review the effectiveness of the company's system of internal control and should report to shareholders. This report should cover all controls, including financial, operational and compliance controls and risk management.

D.4 The directors should report that the business is a going concern, with supporting assumptions or qualifications as necessary.

D.5   Companies which do not have an internal audit
       function should from time to time review the
       need for one.

Principle
Relationship with the auditors. The board should
establish formal and transparent arrangements for
considering how they should apply the financial
reporting and internal control principles and for
maintaining an appropriate relationship with the
company's auditors.

Code provisions
D.6   The board should establish an audit committee
       of at least three non-executive directors with
       written terms of reference which deal clearly
       with its authority and duties. The members of
       the committee, a majority of whom should be
       independent non-executive directors, should be
       named in the report and accounts.

D.7   The duties of the audit committee should
       include keeping under review the scope and
       results of the audit and its cost effectiveness and
       the independence and objectivity of the
       auditors. Where the auditors also supply a
       substantial volume of non-audit services to the
       company, the committee should keep the
       nature and extent of such services under
       review, seeking to balance the maintenance of
       objectivity and value for money.

Section 2 – Institutional shareholders

Principle
Shareholder voting. Institutional shareholders have a
responsibility to make considered use of their votes.

Code provisions
E. 1   Institutional shareholders should endeavour to
       eliminate unnecessary variations in the criteria
       which each applies to the corporate governance
       arrangements and performance of the
       companies in which they invest.

E.2 Institutional shareholders should, on request, make available to their clients information on the proportion of resolutions on which votes were cast and non-discretionary proxies lodged.

E.3 Institutional shareholders should take steps to ensure that their voting intentions are being translated into practice.

Principle
Dialogue with companies. Institutional shareholders should be ready, where practicable, to enter into a dialogue with companies based on the mutual understanding of objectives.

Principle
Evaluation of governance disclosures. When evaluating companies' governance arrangements, particularly those relating to board structure and composition, institutional investors should give due weight to all relevant factors drawn to their attention.

SCHEDULE A: PROVISIONS ON THE DESIGN OF PERFORMANCE RELATED REMUNERATION

1   Remuneration committees should consider whether the directors should be eligible for annual bonuses. If so, performance conditions should be relevant, stretching and designed to enhance the business. Upper limits should always be considered. There may be a case for part payment in shares to be held for a significant period.

2   Remuneration committees should consider whether the directors should be eligible for benefits under long-term incentive schemes. Traditional share option schemes should be weighed against other kinds of long-term incentive scheme. In normal circumstances, shares granted or other forms of deferred remuneration should not vest, and options should not be exercisable, in under three years. Directors should be encouraged to hold their

shares for a further period after vesting or exercise subject to the need to finance any costs of acquisition and associated tax liability.

3   Any new long-term incentive schemes which are proposed should be approved by shareholders and should preferably replace schemes or at least form part of a well-considered overall plan, incorporating existing schemes. The total rewards potentially available should not be excessive.

4   Payouts or grants under all incentive schemes, including new grants under existing share option schemes, should be subject to challenging performance criteria reflecting the company's objectives. Consideration should be given to criteria which reflect the company's performance relative to a group of comparator companies in some key variables such as total shareholder return.

5   Grants under executive share option and other long-term incentive schemes should normally be phased rather than awarded in one large block.

6   Remuneration committees should consider the pension consequences and associated costs to the company of basic salary increases and other changes in remuneration, especially for directors close to retirement.

7   In general, neither annual bonuses nor benefits in kind should be pensionable.

SCHEDULE B: PROVISIONS ON WHAT SHOULD BE INCLUDED IN THE REMUNERATION REPORT

1   The report should include full details of all elements in the remuneration package of each individual director by name, such as basic salary, benefits in kind, annual bonuses and long-term incentive schemes including share options.

2   Information on share options, including SAVE options, should be given for each

director in accordance with the recommendations of the Accounting Standards Board's Urgent Issues Task Force Abstract 10 and its successors.

3   If grants under executive share option or other long-term incentive schemes are awarded in one large block rather than phased, the report should explain and justify.

4   Also included in the report should be pension entitlements earned by each individual director during the year, calculated on one of the alternative bases recommended by the Faculty of Actuaries and the Institute of Actuaries and included in the Stock Exchange Listing Rules. Companies should make clear that transfer values cannot meaningfully be added to annual remuneration.

5   If annual bonuses or benefits in kind are pensionable the report should explain and justify.

6   The amounts received by, and commitments made to, each director under 1, 2 and 4 above should be subject to audit.

7   Any service contracts which provide for, or imply, notice periods in excess of one year (or any provisions for predetermined compensation on termination which exceed one year's salary and benefits) should be disclosed and the reasons for the longer notice periods explained.

5 Board guidelines on significant corporate governance issues: the General Motors case

In 1994 the General Motors board re-examined its processes and established a set of operating guidelines to ensure that it was performing its responsibilities with the same discipline and dedication that it expects of management.

The following guidelines for the board were revised in August 1995.

Selection and composition of the board

1 Board membership criteria
The committee on director affairs is responsible for reviewing with the board, on an annual basis, the appropriate skills and characteristics required of board members in the context of the current make-up of the board. This assessment should include issues of diversity, age, skills such as understanding of manufacturing technologies, international background, etc – all in the context of an assessment of the perceived needs of the board at that point in time.

2 Selection and orientation of new directors
The board itself should be responsible, in fact as well as procedure, for selecting its own members and in recommending them for election by the stockholders. The board delegates the screening process involved to the committee on director affairs with the direct input from the chairman of the board as well as the chief executive officer. The board and the company have a complete orientation process for new directors that includes background material, meetings with senior management and visits to company facilities.

3 Extending the invitation to a potential director to join the board
The invitation to join the board should be

extended by the board itself, by the chairman of the committee on director affairs (if the chairman and chief executive officer hold the same position), the chairman of the board, and the chief executive officer of the company.

Board leadership

4 Selection of chairman and chief executive officer

The board should be free to make this choice any way that seems best for the company at a given point in time. Therefore, the board does not have a policy, one way or the other, on whether or not the role of the chief executive and chairman should be separate and, if it is to be separate, whether the chairman should be selected from the non-employee directors or be an employee.

5 Lead director concept

The board adopted a policy that it have a director selected by the outside directors who will assume the responsibility of chairing the regularly scheduled meetings of outside directors or other responsibilities which the outside directors as a whole might designate from time to time. Currently, this role is filled by the non-executive chairman of the board. Should the company be organised in such a way that the chairman is an employee of the company, another director would be selected for this responsibility.

Board composition and performance

6 Size of the board

The board presently has 13 members. It is the sense of the board that a size of about 15 is about right. However, the board would be willing to go to a larger size in order to accommodate the availability of an outstanding candidate(s).

7 Mix of inside and outside directors

The board believes that as a matter of policy there should be a majority of independent directors on the GM board (as stipulated in Bylaw 2.12). The board is willing to have members of management, in addition to the chief executive officer, as directors. But the board believes that management should encourage senior managers to understand that board membership is not necessary or a prerequisite to any higher management position in the company. Managers other than the chief executive officer currently attend board meetings on a regular basis even though they are not members of the board. On matters of corporate governance, the board assumes decisions will be made by the outside directors.

8 Board definition of what constitutes independence for outside directors

GM's Bylaw defining independent directors was approved by the board in January 1991. The board believes there is no current relationship between any outside director at GM that would be construed in any way to compromise any board member being designated independent. Compliance with the Bylaw is reviewed annually by the committee on director affairs.

9 Former chief executive officer's board membership

The board believes this is a matter to be decided in each individual instance. It is assumed that when the chief executive officer resigns from that position, he/she should offer his/her resignation from the board at the same time. Whether the individual continues to serve on the board is a matter for discussion at that time with the new chief executive officer and the board. A former chief executive officer serving on the board will be considered an inside director for purposes of corporate governance.

10 Directors who change their present job responsibility

It is the sense of the board that individual directors who change the responsibility they held when they were elected to the board should submit a letter of resignation to the board. It is not the sense of the board that in every instance the directors who retire or change from the position they held when they came on the board should necessarily leave the board. There should, however, be an opportunity for the board, via the committee on director affairs, to review the continued appropriateness of board membership under these circumstances.

11 Term limits

The board does not believe it should establish term limits. While term limits could help insure that there are fresh ideas and viewpoints available to the board, they hold the disadvantage of losing the contribution of directors who have been able to develop, over a period of time, increasing insight into the company and its operations and, therefore, provide an increasing contribution to the board as a whole. As an alternative to term limits, the committee on director affairs, in conjunction with the chief executive officer and the chairman of the board, will formally review each director's continuation on the board every five years. This will also allow each director the opportunity to conveniently confirm his/her desire to continue as a member of the board.

12 Retirement age

It is the sense of the board that the current retirement age of 70 is appropriate.

13 Board compensation review

It is appropriate for the staff of the company to report once a year to the committee on director affairs the status of GM board compensation in relation to other large US companies. As part of a director's total compensation and to create a direct linkage with corporate performance, the board believes that a meaningful portion of a director's compensation should be provided in common stock units. Changes in board compensation, if any, should come at the suggestion of the committee on director affairs, but with full discussion and concurrence by the board.

14 Executive sessions of outside directors
The outside directors of the board will meet in executive session three times each year. The format of these meetings will include a discussion with the chief executive officer on each occasion.

15 Assessing the board's performance
The committee on director affairs is responsible to report annually to the board an assessment of the board's performance. This will be discussed with the full board. This should be done following the end of each fiscal year and at the same time as the report on board membership criteria. This assessment should be of the board's contribution as a whole and specifically review areas in which the board and/or the management believes a better contribution could be made. Its purpose is to increase the effectiveness of the board, not to target individual board members.

16 Board interaction with institutional investors, the press, customers, etc
The board believes that the management speaks for General Motors. Individual board members may, from time to time at the request of the management, meet or otherwise communicate with various constituencies that are involved with General Motors. If comments from the board are appropriate, they should, in most circumstances, come from the chairman.

Board relationship to senior management

17 Regular attendance of non-directors at board meetings
The board welcomes the regular attendance at each board meeting of non-board members who are members of the president's council. Should the chief executive officer want to add additional people as attendees on a regular basis, it is expected that this suggestion would be made to the board for its concurrence.

18 Board access to senior management

Board members have complete access to GM's management. It is assumed that board members will use judgment to be sure that this contact is not distracting to the business operation of the company and that such contact, if in writing, be copied to the chief executive and the chairman. Furthermore, the board encourages the management to, from time to time, bring managers into board meetings who: (a) can provide additional insight into the items being discussed because of personal involvement in these areas; and/or (b) represent managers with future potential that the senior management believes should be given exposure to the board.

Meeting procedures

19 Selection of agenda items for board meetings

The chairman of the board and the chief executive officer (if the chairman is not the chief executive officer) will establish the agenda for each board meeting. Each board member is free to suggest the inclusion of item(s) on the agenda.

20 Board materials distributed in advance

It is the sense of the board that information and data that is important to the board's understanding of the business be distributed in writing to the board before the board meets. The management will make every attempt to see that this material is as brief as possible while still providing the desired information.

21 Board presentations

As a general rule, presentations on specific subjects should be sent to the board members in advance so that board meeting time may be conserved and discussion time focused on questions that the board has about the material. On those occasions in which the subject matter is too sensitive to put on paper, the presentation will be discussed at the meeting.

Committee matters

22 Number, structure and independence of committees

The current committee structure of the company seems appropriate. There will, from time to time, be occasions on which the board may want to form a new committee or disband a current committee depending upon the circumstances. The current six committees are audit, capital stock, director affairs, finance, executive compensation and public policy. The committee membership, with the exception of the finance committee, will consist only of independent directors as stipulated in Bylaw 2.12.

23 Assignment and rotation of committee members

The committee on director affairs is responsible, after consultation with the chief executive officer and with consideration of the desires of individual board members, for the assignment of board members to various committees. It is the sense of the board that consideration should be given to rotating committee members periodically at about a five-year interval, but the board does not feel that such a rotation should be mandated as a policy since there may be reasons at a given point in time to maintain an individual director's committee membership for a longer period.

24 Frequency and length of committee meetings

The committee chairman, in consultation with committee members, will determine the frequency and length of the meetings of the committee.

25 Committee agenda

The chairman of the committee, in consultation with the appropriate members of management and staff, will develop the committee's agenda. Each committee will issue a schedule of agenda subjects to be discussed for the ensuing year at the beginning of each year (to the degree these can be foreseen). This forward agenda will also be shared with the board.

Leadership development

26 Formal evaluation of the chief executive officer

The full board (outside directors) should make this evaluation annually, and it should be communicated to the chief executive officer by the (non-executive) chairman of the board or the lead director. The evaluation should be based on objective criteria including performance of the business, accomplishment of long-term strategic objectives, development of management, etc. The evaluation will be used by the executive compensation committee in the course of its deliberations when considering the compensation of the chief executive officer.

27 Succession planning

There should be an annual report by the chief executive officer to the board on succession planning. There should also be available, on a continuing basis, the chief executive officer's recommendation as to a successor should he/she be unexpectedly disabled.

28 Management development

There should be an annual report to the board by the chief executive officer on the company's programme for management development. This report should be given to the board at the same time as the succession planning report noted previously.

Grateful thanks are extended to the chairman and the board of General Motors for permission to reproduce these board guidelines.

6 Audit committee proforma charter

An audit committee needs to have clear terms of reference which define its purpose, authority, membership and chairmanship; the frequency of and attendance at meetings; and its duties. The following charter, adapted to the specific governance circumstances in a company, can provide a basis for the development of an audit committee.

Purpose

The audit committee is a standing committee of the board of directors, to provide a board-level link between the independent external auditors and the board. Its functions include advising the board on the systems of internal management control and on matters of internal audit; liaising with the external auditors and reporting to the board on the audit process and on any audit issues; reviewing financial information to be provided to shareholders and others, and advising the board on matters of board accountability.

Authority

The audit committee has the power to authorise and conduct whatever meetings, interviews or investigations it deems necessary. It may seek information directly from any company employee, although normally this should be done with the knowledge of the chief executive officer or finance director. The head of the internal audit function reports directly to the chairman of the audit committee. The committee may obtain independent accounting, legal or other professional advice in pursuit of its responsibilities.

Membership and chairmanship

The audit committee shall consist of not less than three and not more than five independent non-executive directors, the quorum being two. The chairman of the audit committee shall be appointed by the board.

Meeting frequency

The audit committee shall meet whenever it deems necessary with a minimum of three times a year (typically before, during and at the conclusion of the external audit process). The external auditors may also request a meeting with the audit committee if they deem it necessary.

Meeting participation

Typically the finance director (or chief financial officer), the internal auditor and a representative of the external auditors will attend meetings of the audit committee. Other executive directors or members of management may be asked to attend if necessary. The audit committee may meet separately with the external auditor, the internal auditor, other directors or members of management if they wish to raise matters privately with the committee. At least once a year, the audit committee will meet the external auditor without any members of management being present. The external auditors will also meet the entire board at least once a year and be available to answer questions at shareholders' meetings.

Duties

The audit committee's responsibilities include the duty to:

1 Liaise between the external auditor, the internal auditor and the board as a whole.
2 Advise on the appointment, reappointment, resignation, replacement of the external auditor.
3 Ensure the independence of the external auditor, reviewing the extent of non-audit work undertaken and the fees involved.
4 Review the audit fees and advise the board accordingly.
5 Consider the scope of the work and plans of the external audit.
6 Consider the scope of the work and plans of the internal audit. Supervise the work of the head of the internal audit function, including the setting of policies, procedures and plans, the budgeting of

resources, the remuneration and performance of staff, the regular monitoring of results and the overall effectiveness of the function.

7 Ensure that the activities of the external and internal auditors are co-ordinated, avoiding either duplication or incomplete coverage.

8 Review the appointment, performance, remuneration and replacement or dismissal of the head of the internal audit function, ensuring continuing independence of the internal audit function from undue managerial influence.

9 Review with the external and internal auditors and advise the board on the adequacy of the company's internal control systems, security of physical assets and protection of information.

10 Review with the external and internal auditors and advise the board on the conduct of the external audit, particularly any important findings or matters raised, usually contained in the auditor's management letter, with management's response; and report any significant changes to the reporting of financial results or to procedures and management controls that resulted.

11 Review with the external and internal auditors and advise the board on the company's financial statements (interim and annual) prior to publication, the auditor's report to the shareholders, any changes to accounting policies, material issues arising in or from the financial statements; and compliance with accounting standards, company law (and if appropriate stock exchange) reporting requirements and corporate governance codes of good practice.

12 Review any other published information, such as the directors' report, and ensure that it is consistent with the audited financial statements.

13 Review the exposure of the company to risk and any matters that might have a material effect on the company's financial position, including any matters raised by company regulators or stock exchange listing committees.

14 Review annually the charter of the audit committee and advise the chairman of the board if changes are necessary.

7 Sources of information for directors around the world

PROFESSIONAL ORGANISATIONS FOR DIRECTORS

Australia
Australian Institute of Company Directors
National president: J.T. Ralph
CEO: Ian T Dunlop
3F 71 York Street, Sydney, NSW 2000
Tel: +612 9299 8788

Canada
The Institute of Corporate Directors
Chairman: T.H. Savage
CEO: Mrs L. Oler
Tel: +1 416 944 8282

Hong Kong
The Hong Kong Institute of Directors
Chairman: Moses Mo-Chi Cheng
Tel: +852 2867 1185

New Zealand
The Institute of Directors of New Zealand
President: Basil Logan
CEO: David Newman
Tel: +644 499 0076

Nigeria
The Institute of Directors
Chairman: Alhaji A.O.G. Otiti
Director general: Mrs O. Obada
Tel: +2341 269 4015

South Africa
The Institute of Directors in Southern Africa
President: Basil E. Hersov
Chairman: Adv. S. Tucker
Executive director: R.S. Wilkinson
Tel: +2711 643 8086

UK
The Institute of Directors
President: The Rt. Hon Lord Young
Director general: Tim Melville-Ross
116 Pall Mall, London, SW1Y 5ED
Tel: +44 171 839 1233

The Institute of Directors
Centre for Director Development
Director of professional development: John Harper
Tel: +44 171 766 8800
Web site: http://www.iod.co.uk

United States
National Association of Corporate Directors
Suite 560, 1701 L Street NW, Washington, DC 20036
Tel: +1 202 775 0509

**DISTANCE LEARNING PROGRAMMES FOR
DIRECTORS**

Australia
The Australian Institute of Company Directors
See above

The University of New England
Armidale, NSW 2351
Tel: +61 67 732480

UK
**Leeds Metropolitan University/The Institute
of Directors/FT Management**
For information contact Institute of Directors

**DIRECTOR AND CORPORATE GOVERNANCE
JOURNALS**

Hong Kong
Corporate Governance International
Editor: John Brewer
Sweet and Maxwell, Suite 1808, Asian House,
1 Hennessy Road, Wanchai, Hong Kong
Tel: +852 2863 2635

UK
Corporate Governance – an international review
Editor: Dr R.I. (Bob) Tricker
Blackwell Publishers, 108, Cowley Road, Oxford
OX4 1JF
Tel: +44 1865 791 100
Web site: http://www.BlackwellPublishers.co.uk
Blackwell Publishers, 238 Main Street, Suite 501,
Cambridge MA 02142
Tel: +1 617 547 7110
Research and practice journal, quarterly, now in
its seventh year

The Director
Editor: Tom Nash
Director Publications, Mountbarrow House,
Elizabeth Street, London SW1W 9RB
Tel: +44 171 730 6060
Professional journal, monthly

Governance
Editor: Matthew Gaved
Gee Publishing, 100 Avenue Road, Swiss Cottage,
London NW3 3PG
Tel: +44 171 393 7400
Newsletter, monthly

United States
Directors and Boards
229 South 18th Street, Philadelphia, PA 19103-9827
Journal, monthly, now in its 21st year

Global Proxy Watch
Davis Global Advisers, 57 Hancock Street,
Newton, MA 02166
Tel: +1 617 630 8792
Newsletter, faxed weekly

The Corporate Board
Editor: Ralph D. Ward
6604 W. Saginaw Highway, Lansing, MI 48917
Tel. +1 517 321 0667
Journal bi-monthly

OTHER RELEVANT ORGANISATIONS

UK
The Centre for Board Effectiveness
President: Sir Adrian Cadbury
Director: Professor Bernard Taylor
Henley Management Centre, Greenlands,
Henley-on-Thames, RG9 3AU
Tel: +44 1491 571 454

United States
Investor Responsibility Research Centre
1350 Connecticut Avenue NW, Washington, DC
20036-1701
Tel: +1 202 833 0700

Institutional Shareholder Services
7200 Wisconsin Avenue, Suite 1001, Bethesda,
Maryland, 20811
Tel: +1 301 718 2255

CORPORATE GOVERNANCE WEB SITES

There is now a lot of material relevant to corporate governance and the work of directors on the Internet and it is increasing daily. An excellent starting point for discussions of current frontier topics in corporate governance, information on the work of boards and links to many other related web sites including corporate governance centres, institutional and relational investors and related topics, is at http://www.corpgov.net

Another worthwhile site by the relationship investor the Lens Fund is at:
http://www.lens-inc.com

8 Recommended reading

Berle, A. and Means, G., *The Modern Corporation and Private Property*, Macmillan, New York, 1932. The first and most frequently quoted study of corporate governance.

Bosch, Henry, *The Director at Risk – accountability in the boardroom*, Pitman Publishing, Australia, 1995.

Brancato, Carolyn Kay, *Institutional Investors and Corporate Governance – best practices for increasing corporate value*, The Conference Board and McGraw Hill, New York, 1997.

Cadbury, Sir Adrian (chairman), *The Report of the Committee on the Financial Aspects of Corporate Governance*, Gee and Co, London, 1992.

Charkham, Jonathan, *Keeping Good Company – a study of corporate governance in five countries*, Oxford University Press, Oxford, 1994.

Clarke, Thomas, "Measuring and managing shareholder relations", *Journal of Communications Management*, Vol. 3, No. 3, March 1998.

Demb, Ada and Neubauer, Fred, *The Corporate Board – confronting the paradoxes*, Oxford University Press, New York, 1992.

Egon Zehnder, *Chairmen and non-executive directors – fees, facts and attitudes 1996*, with ProNed and the Institute of Chartered Accountants in England and Wales, 1996.

Fama, Eugene and Jensen, Michael, "Separation of Ownership and Control", *Journal of Law and Economics*, Vol. 26, June 1983. A classic on agency theory.

Garratt, Bob, *The Fish Rots from the Head – the crisis in our boardrooms: developing the crucial skills of the competent director*, HarperCollins, London, 1997.

Greenbury, Sir Richard (chairman), *The Report of the Committee on Directors' Remuneration*, Gee and Co, London, 1995.

Hampel Report, Committee on Corporate Governance, London, January 1998.

Handy, Charles, "What is a company for?", *Corporate Governance – an international review*, Vol. 1, No. 1, January 1993.

Hawley, James P. and Williams, Andrew T., "Corporate Governance in the United States – the rise of fiduciary capitalism – a review of the literature", *OECD background paper*. First prize in Lens Corporate Governance papers competition 1997.

Hilmer, Frederick G. (chairman), *Strictly Ballroom – improving governance to enrich company performance*, a study facilitated by The Sydney Institute, Information Australia, Melbourne, VIC, Australia, 1993.

Hilmer Frederick G. and Tricker, Robert I., "Board effectiveness", in *The Australian Company Director's Handbook*, Australian Institute of Company Directors, Sydney, Australia 1991.

Hopt, Klaus J. and Wymeersch, Eddy, *Comparative Corporate Governance – essays and materials*, de Gruyter, Berlin, 1997.

Hutton, Will and others, *Stake-holding and its Critics*, The IEA Health and Welfare Unit, 2 North Street, London SW1P 3LB, 1997.

Institute of Chartered Accountants in England and Wales – Audit Faculty, Audit Committees – a framework for assessment, May 1997.

Institute of Directors, *Good Practice for Directors – standards for the board*, Institute of Directors, 116 Pall Mall, London, SW1 5ED, 1995.

International Capital Markets Group, *International Corporate Governance – who holds the reins?*, ICMG, c/o International Bar Association, Hanover Square, London, June 1995.

Millstein, Ira M. and Katsch, Salem M., *The Limits of Corporate Power – existing constraints on the exercise of corporate discretion*, Collier-Macmillan, New York, 1981.

Monks, Robert A. G, *The Emperor's Nightingale – how the emerging dynamics of corporate complexity will restore integrity to economic lie in the new millennium*, working manuscript, 1200 G Street NW, Washington, DC 20005, USA, 1997.

Netherlands Committee on Corporate Governance, *Corporate Governance in the Netherlands, Forty recommendations for sound management, effective supervision and accountability*, Amsterdam, June 1997.

Price Waterhouse, *Audit Committees – a study in European corporate governance*, with the Community of European Management Schools, September 1997.

Royal Society of Arts, *RSA Inquiry – Tomorrow's Company*, April 1995.

Russell Reynolds, *Setting new standards for corporate governance – 1997 US survey of institutional investors*, 1997.

Sun Tse, *The Art of War*, Bamboo sticks, c. 600 BC. Available in an number of English translations and commentaries.

Tricker, R.I., *Corporate Governance*, Gower, Aldershot, 1984.

Tricker, R.I., *International Corporate Governance – text, readings and cases*, Prentice Hall, Singapore, 1994.

Turnbull, Shann, "Shareholder democracy – redesigning the governance of firms and bureaucracies", *The Journal of Socio-Economics*, Vol. 32, No. 9, 1994.